REFUTING ISIS

REFUTING ISIS

DESTROYING ITS RELIGIOUS FOUNDATIONS AND
PROVING THAT IT HAS STRAYED FROM ISLAM AND
THAT FIGHTING IT IS AN OBLIGATION

BY
Shaykh Muhammad Al-Yaqoubi

Sacred
KNOWLEDGE

I dedicate this book to the innocent Syrians
who have been unjustly killed in the name of Islam.
I pray that Allah Almighty accepts them with His
Infinite Mercy and Forgiveness
and grants their families patience and comfort.

Contents

Honorific Phrases in Arabic

ﷺ (*Salla-llahu 'alayhi wa sallam*) an invocation of Allah's blessings and peace upon the Prophet Muhammad: "Allah's blessings and peace be upon him"

ﷺ: (*'Alayhis-salam*) an invocation of Allah's blessings and peace upon a Prophet or an angel: "May peace be upon him"

ﷺ (*'Alayhimus-salam*) an invocation of Allah's blessings and peace upon three or more Prophets: "May peace be upon them"

ﷺ (*Radiyallahu 'anhu*) an invocation of Allah's pleasure with a male Companion of the Prophet: "May Allah be pleased with him"

ﷺ (*Radiyallahu 'anha*) an invocation of Allah's pleasure with a female Companion of the Prophet: "May Allah be pleased with her"

ﷺ (*Radiyallahu 'anhuma*) an invocation of Allah's pleasure with a two Companions of the Prophet: "May Allah be pleased with both of them"

Preface

ISLAM HAS NEVER been challenged from the inside as it is being now. Scholars are therefore obliged to respond, and their response should be intellectual. The ideology of ISIS is based on a complex system of fallacies that cut the sacred texts from their context, and on a series of devious stratagems that select from the corpus of the law what satisfies their twisted minds.

There is a plethora of proofs to destroy the allegations of ISIS and expose their manipulation of the Shariah (Islamic law), but knowledge of these proofs is confined to the classical texts and is generally inaccessible to the average Muslim reader.

From recognizing this void sprung forth the idea of writing this book—to offer a handbook that clarifies the position of Sunni Islam towards ISIS and its atrocities. It is also the first attempt to intellectually defy ISIS, not only by offering a decisive rebuttal to their feeble narrative but also by defining the theological standing of the group and the legal status of their self-declared caliphate. This book proceeds through a series of carefully constructed arguments, proving that the so-called "Islamic State" is neither Islamic nor a state, but rather a deviant group of gangsters driven by anger, hatred, and a thirst for power, using Islam as a pretense to reach their goals.

This book was written in February 2015 and first published first in Arabic in June of the same year. I subsequently rendered the book into English. Although it is an advantage for any author to translate his own work, there is always the appetite to expand the original text, especially when the audience or the style dictates so. Nevertheless, I maintained the same order of chapters and quotes, but added a few points which were raised in a recent interview about the status of religious minorities under Islamic governance, specifically as to whether they must embrace Islam or face execution, or, according to the majority of the jurists, maintain their beliefs and be citizens in their countries, living peacefully side by side with Muslims and other groups.

Refuting ISIS is aimed at five different groups: (1) Muslim youth who are being influenced by the propaganda of ISIS, with no alternative rejoinders (2) Common Muslims who are seeking answers to the new theological and legal challenges brought by ISIS (3) New recruits within ISIS, to help them defect by proving to them that ISIS has strayed from Islam and that the oath of allegiance to its leader is void (4) The fighters of the Free Syrian Army (FSA) in Syria, the Muslim pilots from the alliances against ISIS, and their families, as many of them are wondering about the legitimacy of war against their "Muslim brothers" and whether they die as martyrs for a just cause. Some FSA brigades were hesitating in their fight against ISIS, but after it was explained to them some of what has been included in this book, they became firmly convinced that fighting ISIS is a religious obligation. This group benefitted from the Arabic version of the book. (5) The western audience, academics, journalists, politicians, and the public, the majority of whom have always admired Islam as a set of tenets and a religion of peace and civility, but when faced with the practices of ISIS, took pause as they wondered where the Muslim scholars are and why they are silent. Many in the West have heard Muslim figures in the media disassociating true Islam from the actions of ISIS, however for intellectuals that in itself was not convincing enough; the voice of an expert and scholar was required in order to dig out the treasures of the Islamic legal system and present proofs which undeniably refute the allegations of ISIS and demonstrate its fallacies.

There are several elements in the ideology of ISIS that contribute to its extremist views and practices. Some may be derived from Sayyid Qutb's works and the hard-line Muslim Brotherhood (MB) movement; some may have stemmed from the Salafi movement, which gave birth to what is known today as Jihadi Salafism. Nonetheless, I have not engaged in tracing the origins of ISIS' ideology, as this work does not aim to present a historical study or a political analysis. Our work is an attempt to present the views of Sunni Islam, the religion of the majority of Muslims in the world today, concerning the challenges presented by ISIS, presenting views which are supported by classical texts and major works in the corpus of Islamic law.

Salafism in itself is of two types: (1) Salafism in dogma, which constitutes an independent theological school, with Ibn Taymiyya as its leading ideologue, whose beliefs tend toward anthropomorphism; and (2) Salafism in law (*fiqh*), which is characterized by rebelling against the four Sunni schools of Islamic law (*madhabs*) and calling people to consider the Quran and the Prophetic Traditions as the only sources of legislation, thus discarding the legacy of the four schools and their centuries of scholarship, at times going to the extent of ridiculing their adherents. The Salafi movement was strengthened in the late 19th and early 20th centuries by Muhammad Abduh (d. 1905) and Rashid Rida (d. 1935). Saudi Arabia strictly follows the Hanbali school, so its Salafism is limited to theology while recognizing the other three schools of law. ISIS, on the other hand, rebels against all of the schools of Islamic law, and against most Salafi interpretations, while adhering to Ibn Taymiyya in his theological views. This lack of an authority in legislation, coupled with the absence of a major reference or manual of law in the hands of ISIS' judges and Shariah personnel, has led almost every fighter placed in charge of a situation to present a contrived legal ruling based on his own understanding of the Quran and Tradition, most often selecting the quotes which seemingly validate their vengeful ill will. The brutality, savagery, and barbarity we have witnessed from this group is a testimony to the inherent danger of giving ignorant fanatics the authority to do the job of the great independent legal authorities (*mujtahids*), a status which even great figures such as al-Ghazali and al-Nawawi could not claim.

Therefore, we should concede that the extreme practices of ISIS are a direct result of the breaking of the undeclared authority of the Sunni doctors of law. The movement which interrupted their authority has developed for well over a century and has been strengthened by two factors. First, the marginalization of traditional Islam at the hands of secular governments in most parts of the Islamic world (with Morocco being an exception due to the Islamic authority its monarchs assumed over the centuries). Second, the rise of political Islamic movements, which often adopted a Salafist approach in the course of their rebellion against the authority of the 'Ulama (scholars) whom they consider an obstacle to the establishment of their own Islamic state and the classical institutions of Sunni Islam, such as al-Azhar.

Despite the criticism they have received, and despite all of the opinions which may seem irrelevant in today's practice of Islam, the four Sunni schools of law remain the safeguard from the disarray we witness today. There are several reasons for this. First, these schools bear the seed of development as they set forth a group of principles and a collection of governing legal rules which allow them to evolve from within the school itself according to changing conditions in every specific time and place. Imam al-Shafi'i, for example, changed most of his legal opinions when he migrated to Egypt. Furthermore, in every school of law there is the old camp and the new camp whose opinions in many cases may be conflicting. In the Maliki school of law, and specifically, in the works of Imam al-Shatibi, you find the principle of *Maqasid al-Shari'a*, meaning the higher purposes and goals of the law, which give the legislator the authority to even freeze a text and act against it, an example being when the Caliph 'Umar halted the application of the penalty for theft during a year of famine.

It is in these schools that we find the principles and the precedence to counter the extreme practices of ISIS which it attributes to the Shariah. Readers will see in this book several examples to illustrate this point, but let me elaborate here on one specific example regarding Islamic penalties: the Hanafi school of law took the opinion that legal penalties (*hudud*) cannot be implemented in a time of ignorance, and the Shafi'i school of law stated that penalties cannot be implemented if there is fear that the accused may abscond to the enemy or leave Islam entirely.

The readers of this book will see quotes and anecdotes that have never been mentioned or highlighted in our Islamic discourse today. I selected from only the reliable, classical books of law and presented them as samples to show the real character of Islam and its inherent principles of tolerance and mutual respect for all of humanity. In order to refute ISIS and destroy their arguments, I have followed in this book a method of bringing a sounder proof or a more reliable text, which you may call a counter-narrative. I do not engage in detailed discussion and analysis of ISIS' arguments, as this book is meant to be brief, easy to read, and mainly provide ordinary Muslims with strong arguments against ISIS. However, a thorough critical look into ISIS' proofs is complete and was deliberately not included in this book, as it would go against the basic purpose of the book and the ease with which it can be read and understood by every young Muslim.

Introduction

*Praise be to Allah, Lord of the Worlds, and prayers and peace be upon
Our Master Muhammad, the Seal of Prophets, sent as a mercy to the
worlds, and upon his Family and all his Companions.*

A NUMBER OF questions were sent to me in the past few months
regarding the group known as "The Islamic State," to which the media
typically refers with the initials "ISIS," which stands for "The Islamic
State in Iraq and Syria," or "ISIL," which stands for "The Islamic State
in Iraq and the Levant." Seven questions were posed to me:

1. Is the declaration of a caliphate by ISIS valid?
2. Are the crimes of ISIS justified in Islam?
3. Does ISIS represent Sunni Islam?
4. Are Muslims allowed to fight against ISIS?
5. Where does the ideology of ISIS come from?
6. What is Islam's position on fighting ISIS?
7. How do we protect our youth from being brainwashed by
   the ideology of ISIS?

Important questions posed.

A number of brigades in Syria have resorted to fighting against
these extremists, which has distracted many of them from jihad against
the Assad regime, leading to the martyrdom of some amongst them.
Likewise, a number of Muslim nations have declared war against this
notoriously dangerous group. Fighters in Syria and other Arab nations
have also enquired about the ruling of this fighting and the status of
whoever is killed in these battles—particularly, they are asking if they
are martyrs?

For some time, discussions have been taking place in the public sphere
regarding the status of pilots who participate in the war against ISIS, and

while many famous scholars have hesitated in giving a ruling, some did not even consider those killed while fighting ISIS as martyrs—a position which I refute in this book. Similarly, wherever I go, I often field questions from the public about Islam's position regarding the heinous crimes perpetrated by members of this group in the name of Islam. Furthermore, a number of non-Muslims have questioned the stance of Sunni Islam regarding the actions of ISIS. Given the false categorization of ISIS' followers as Sunni Muslims that has been proliferated in the public psyche, many non-Muslims are seeking clarity as to what degree the views and actions of ISIS represent Sunni Islam. The need for clarity is intensified by the fact that a number of western media outlets jump at the opportunity to promote a false equivalency between the ideology of ISIS and the position of mainstream Muslims, a prominent example being Fox News. These media outlets have found substantial material in this group's fatwas, stances, and crimes to promote a fear of Islam amongst the western masses, in a time where the tide of moderate Islam in the west is rising, as is the number of those entering the faith.

Due to the gravity of the subject and my obligation to expound upon the ruling of Allah Almighty concerning it, I have compiled this concise book and made it a detailed fatwa explaining the legal ruling of fighting the Khawarij generally and ISIS specifically. Through systematically constructed arguments and proofs, I derive the conclusions that ISIS' actions are in complete contradiction to the Shariah, that their claims to a caliphate are invalid, and that fighting against them is a legal obligation for those in the region in order to dismantle their criminal entity.

The Khawarij are a sect which appeared in the first century of Islam and have manifested throughout the centuries since. It deviated from mainstream Islam and was known for killing Muslims under allegations of *takfir,* which means accusing a Muslim of becoming an apostate. This sect was described in numerous Prophetic Traditions (hadith), which I detail in the second chapter of this book. According to the words of Prophet Muhammad ﷺ, the followers the Khawarij are described as "the dogs of Hell," and "the worst of both men and animals." Although the historical sect of the Khawarij does not exist today, we have clear proofs in the Prophetic Traditions that it would emerge at various times throughout the centuries of Islam. The comparison between the crimes and practices of ISIS and the description of the Khawarij mentioned in the words (hadith) of the Prophet proves my conclusion that ISIS is the modern-day Khawarij, implying that its followers are deviators and that fighting them is obligatory.

It is important to note at this juncture that the oath of allegiance to al-Baghdadi is void, as I shall demonstrate. This group, despite being called a state, is not a state from a Shariah point of view, and irrespective of its attribution to Islam it has no connection to it.

ISIS uses Islam and fanciful notions of jihad to recruit the youth and deceive Muslims around the world who feel oppressed by conjuring dreams of establishing an Islamic State from China to the Atlantic that would protect their interests. The question is, do ISIS' followers not realize that their mission is impossible to achieve? The answer is clearly no, because they live in a world of false prophecies and delusions, believing a miracle will enable them to emerge victorious. For this reason, they are happy to destabilize the region, tear Syria and Iraq apart, draw the USA into a military intervention, and provoke Iran.

By fighting the world, they have an underlying goal that we should never allow to happen: to provoke the West against the Muslim world, thus giving legitimacy to their fight and an impetus for angry Muslims to join their cause. Several Western governments have been aware of this fact, as evidenced in the words of many high level officials and policy experts.[1]

It is also worth drawing the reader's attention to the overwhelming suspicion surrounding this group, its instigators, its alliances, and its objectives. Who is behind ISIS? How did it succeed in dominating Mosul and Ramadi? Why does it target the militias fighting the Assad regime in Syria? Why is it attempting to eradicate any history in the region through demolishing relics? Why is it propelling minorities to migrate from the region? Why is it persecuting Sunni Muslims? Why is it sparking hatred between sects and sowing dissension between clans that have lived harmoniously for centuries?[2] Why is it making deals with the same Syrian regime that it professes to oppose?[3]

These are all questions that raise significant doubt and suspicion, emphasizing the point that perhaps there are nefarious strategists behind the rise of ISIS, and that Islam is nothing but a cloak worn by this group to fulfil ulterior motives, thereby distorting the image of Islam in the public conscious and portraying it as a barbaric religion far removed from civilization, humanity, mercy, and justice. [Unsurprisingly, testimonies have been uncovered that disclose the extent of al-Baghdadi's ignorance of Islamic law, his extremism, and his incompetence.]

al-Baghdadi's incompetence

I have concluded by explaining some of the necessary legal rulings linked to Muslims in treaty countries and non-Muslims in Muslim countries. In this context, I have further uncovered this group's public contravention of the Shariah and its deliberate distortion of Islam by violating contracts, deceiving foreign visitors to Syria who must be protected, and terrorizing the population at large.

I have aimed for brevity as much as possible, for the goal of this book is to be easy to read, easy to digest, and easily circulated to allow the masses to benefit from it. I avoided detail in a number of issues where further depth can be found in other publications.

[One of the most important intentions of this book is to clarify the position of the Shariah in contradistinction to the distortions made by the extremists and the ignorant, just as Allah Almighty obligates us to do.]For this reason, I have endeavoured to explain away any ambiguities by presenting appropriate evidences in every instance from the Quran, the Sunna, and the words of the jurists.

most important intention of book

Another primary intention behind this book is to educate and rescue innocent young men and women who are deceived into travelling from various countries to join ISIS. They come with idealized dreams of an Islamic state that are abruptly shattered when they behold a contemptible gang of criminals. Many of them eventually try to flee from this group's dictatorship. They are encouraged to repent and return to their roots, for the repentant are like the sinless.

I have closely followed the proofs this group has published and disseminated, such as the book entitled, *Informing Mankind of the Emergence of the Islamic State*, so that I do not err in my fatwa or issue an unjust ruling. [We know what they claim and what they have been accused of, so I have distinguished between what they say and what is said regarding them. Conceptualization takes precedence over the verdict; the former is the foundation while the latter is a branch of it. Al-Akhdari said:

> *The perception of a single meaning is called conception*
> *The perception of the relation between two is known as judgement*
> *The first should always be mentioned before the second*
> *Because it naturally precedes it*

I have read the books and proofs penned in refutation of this group, some of which are written by scholars of the Salafi-Jihadi movement. I have used their statements as proofs to substantiate my conclusions further, albeit not as a basis of my arguments.

Based on the obligation to raise public awareness, I call on sermonizers, preachers, and teachers in mosques and institutions in Syria and across the world to explain these rulings to the masses. It is an obligation to shed light on these ambiguities, and impermissible to leave people exposed to uncertainties and doubts on grave issues of this nature.

ISIS is instigating a vast propaganda campaign and justifying the heinous crimes it is committing under the pretext of supporting Islam and implementing the Shariah, thereby attracting the hearts of many of the laity. Every imam, speaker, and teacher of faith in Islamic institutions and colleges carries a responsibility before Allah Almighty to rescue them from the clutches of disbelief, misguidance, death, and destruction.

Likewise, I urge the media to spread this fatwa, communicate its contents, and establish seminars on television and radio to discuss the explanations and clarifications provided herein.

Lest despair arise over the proliferation of this criminal group, I bear glad tidings to Muslims that victory over these Khawarij is imminent. Whoever dies at the hands of this group is the best of martyrs, and whoever remains patient shall be rewarded and shall witness victory. Islam has endured many malevolent groups, trials, and calamities throughout history, and through its justice and mercy, as well as its adherence to the pious scholars and righteous believers, it has prevailed.

The strength of Muslims is not in their numbers or material resources, as proven by the words of Allah Almighty, ❨And on the day of Hunayn:

behold! Your great numbers elated you, but they availed you naught (9:25), but rather in their belief, humility, and obedience to Allah Almighty and their submission to Him. This was the state of the Muslims in the battle of Badr and Allah Almighty said regarding them, *Truly Allah helped you at Badr, when you were a contemptible little force* (3:123).

The pious predecessors of the first generations provided the most superior and relevant example for all posterity: spreading Islam, opening the way for humanity to embrace it, and establishing a civilization—not by force, compulsion, or oppression, but rather by showing good character. Their excellence in conduct was rooted in being truthful in their interaction with non-Muslims, fulfilling their promises, establishing justice even when challenged, threatened, or defeated, and showing mercy to enemies before showing it to friends. In their example we find the culmination of sincerity and God-consciousness filling their hearts, mercy dwelling in their chests, and justice governing their intellects. Their model exemplifies the power of belief when coupled with good character.

When our pious predecessors took the Messenger of Allah ﷺ as their role model in worship and conduct without separating one aspect from the other, they became great and true leaders who inspired the world. They saw how the Prophet pardoned his enemies after thirteen years of oppression and eight years of wars, including the pardoning of Wahshi, the killer of his own paternal uncle Hamza, and the pardoning of Hind, the lady who chewed Hamza's liver upon his martyrdom. They understood the Prophet's definition of a Muslim when he said, "The perfect Muslim is he from whom others are safe from his tongue and hand." This is how a Muslim is recognized by the rest of humanity and how his or her belief is relevant to the society in which he or she lives.

As time passed and true faith became diluted, some of these principles were forgotten, thus paving the way for small fanatical groups which claimed a monopoly on true Islam to emerge. Others grew disillusioned, partly due to the cultural shock of the West and its ideals, and therefore abandoned their history and neglected their heritage, falling victim to the media's portrayal of Islam as a barbaric religion incompatible with modernity. In the process, we left the unique qualities of our faith, which creates an unbreakable link between the theological and spiritual foundations and the social and ethical conduct expected of its believers, as was demonstrated to us in perfection by our Prophet ﷺ.

Consequently, the Muslim nation as a whole plunged from strength to weakness, from honor to humiliation, from a revered community to one of disrepute. The only cure is to return to the supreme example presented by the Messenger of Allah ﷺ by adhering to his Sunna, embracing his guidance, adorning ourselves with his character, and following his heirs: the pious predecessors and righteous scholars.

The foundational ethics of Islam are based on mercy, wisdom, and justice. The Messenger of Allah ﷺ was only sent with mercy and wisdom. He said, "Allah, the Most Merciful, is merciful only to those who show mercy. Be merciful to all on the Earth and the Master of the Heavens will show mercy to you." Saladin (d. 1193), the famous Muslim ruler at the time of the Crusader invasion during the Middle ages, did not enter the annals of history but for his character, justice, and good conduct with his adversaries during both peace and war.

The Levant shall always remain a cornerstone of Islam, a pillar of the Quran, and a land of saints. Its people, especially the Syrians, will remain content with His divine decree, enduring hardships with patience and ever in a state of gratitude for His apparent and subtle blessings.

> *Cradle of the Quran, swords of Islam*
> *Land of the Abdāl, the nation of Sham*
> *Spring of champions, throughout time*
> *Saladin is calling you!*

No matter how long it takes, victory is near, as promised by Allah Almighty. However, the real question is not when will victory come, but rather, do we deserve it? If we do not, then we should endeavour to fulfil the conditions of victory within ourselves if we hope to witness it around us.

From the very onset of the uprising in Syria, I have exposed the reality of the Assad regime, fought against it, and disapproved of its crimes in public forums and on the Friday pulpit. I have never hesitated in my positions; however, I cannot accept amongst our ranks in the war against this regime anyone who perverts the religion, distorts the reality of jihad, deceives the people of the Levant, steals the fruits of their struggles, and tortures them, especially after the Assad regime mastered torture techniques against its own people for over half a century.

Just as I saw the beginning of the end for the Assad regime, I also see the beginning of the end for this sinister group. This is because their followers are destroying the religion from within, striking at the hearts of Muslims, and replacing the corpus of knowledge, jurisprudence, and principles of legal judgements that have reached us with the words of ignorant men. These men have never smelt the scent of knowledge and have not embodied even the lowest level of piety, and have not tasted humility in obedience towards Allah Almighty. The distance between them and the noble qualities of the Messenger of Allah ﷺ as the distance between the east and the west.

Every science has its own experts, many of whom would spend fifty years reading, revising, researching, teaching and authoring. If they were asked regarding an issue they would stop and ponder. They would not be content with what they acquired throughout their lives, but would persist in contemplation and reflection. They would resolve an issue through revision and research out of fear of Allah Almighty lest they show haste in making a legal judgement or err in giving fatwa.

> *There are people of knowledge who are qualified*
> *Every one of them has an awe-inspiring figure*
> *Everyone admits that he is ignorant*
> *When he is like a vast ocean of knowledge*
> *Due to his silence, you think that such a scholar is ignorant*
> *But he is always like a steady mountain*
> *The moment you ask him a difficult question*
> *You hear the clearest and most enriching answer*

There is no scholar amongst these criminals who is an authority for Muslims, whether in belief, jurisprudence, or legal judgements. There isn't even a student of knowledge amongst them who has taken from trustworthy experts, so how can they embark on issuing fatwas and giving legal verdicts? They pass judgement about killing without a second thought, as though slaughtering humans is easier than slaughtering livestock. Abu Salama ﷺ once asked 'A'isha ﷺ regarding the actions that necessitate a ritual bath (*ghusl*). She responded by saying, "Do you know what you are like, O Abu Salama? You are like the chick who hears the roosters crowing and starts crowing with them." She said this either because he was young or because he delved into something unsuitable for him. So how is it then that we are confronted by a group of youth who are less than beginners in knowledge, yet they readily anathematize Muslims and arbitrarily pass judgements to kill, imprison, kidnap, and loot? To describe them as ignorant is an understatement, as a man may be excused due to ignorance but:

> His ignorance is compound yet
> Evident as he looks like a learner

Sunni Muslims in Iraq have suffered from the injustice of the Maliki regime and the people of Syria have suffered from the terror of the Assad regime. Then came ISIS to increase the injustice and terror, leaving the innocent citizens of Iraq and Syria stranded between two horrific options. I say to those who are exposed to injustice and oppression in Syria or Iraq: Have patience as victory is near. Don't let despair or revenge lead you to being deceived by ISIS and joining it. ISIS only wants to subjugate, enslave and humiliate you by using the name of religion instead of dictatorship or socialism.

O Allah! Bless us with awe of you and piety. Fill our hearts with what pleases you. Enable us to act with knowledge and to conduct ourselves with patience, for truly you are the All-Hearing.

O Allah! Help your oppressed servants. Make us your inheritors and use us to guide humanity, speak the truth, and aid the troubled.

O Allah! Bestow your mercy upon us and upon our martyrs. Cure us and heal our injured. Grace us with your kindness and alleviate the sadness that afflicts us.

O Allah! Amend our situation, put our affairs in order, and unite us.

O Allah! Return the people of Syria to their homes, free us from these depraved criminals, and spread peace and security in our lands.

O Most Merciful! You are most generous.

To conclude, all praise belongs to Allah, Lord of the Worlds.

CHAPTER I

In the Words of ISIS

ISIS QUOTES THE Quran and hadith (narrations of the Prophet ﷺ) in abundance and without any relevance to their own behavior in order to provide Islamic credentials to their wicked actions. What legitimacy does ISIS have without the Islamic rhetorical cover of an alleged Caliphate and a self-proclaimed Caliph? ISIS' actions reflect nothing more than a sectarian, barbaric, and vengeful terrorist organization that bears no relation to the beautiful character and practice of Prophet Muhammad ﷺ. The use of Islamic rhetoric is a tool in order to obtain worldly power and territorial control.

The declaration of the self-claimed Caliphate on June 29, 2015 sufficiently shows the power struggle behind ISIS. The declaration came weeks after the capture of Iraq's second largest city, Mosul, on June 10, months after they had taken al-Raqqa in Syria and al-Anbar in Iraq, and surprisingly some eight years after they established their Islamic State of Iraq (ISI) on October 15, 2006. This is very strange behaviour—why this eight year delay in declaring the ISIS Caliphate? The explanation to this discrepancy lies in the conflict between ISIS and Al-Qaida (AQ). AQ's representative in Syria, Jabhat al-Nusra (JN), was supported by ISI since 2012, and when the latter declared the Islamic State of Iraq and al-Sham (ISIS) on April 8, 2013 and included AQ-JN in their State, a bloody conflict arose between AQ-JN and ISIS. AQ-leader Ayman al-Zawahiri supported AQ-JN against ISIS. Naturally, AQ was more known than ISIS at that time. Accordingly, declaring a Caliphate on June 29, 2014 was the only way ISIS could supersede AQ as the premier jihadi organisation and the continuation of the legacy of Usama Bin Laden—and they could not have claimed this religious legitimacy and reputation without hiding under the Islamic cover and rhetoric of being the Caliphate.

I

Upon ISIS' declaration of the Caliphate, their self-claimed Caliph known as Abu Bakr al-Baghdadi claimed to have established a Caliphate "on the Prophetic methodology." It is equally easy to refute this claim by quoting ISIS' own sources, primarily from their English publication named *Dabiq*. I shall cite quotes from ISIS in this section relating to four themes: 1) ISIS' leaders, 2) ISIS' worldview, 3) ISIS' roadmap and 4) ISIS' view on Muslims, which will suffice to illustrate that ISIS is against the very Prophetic Methodology they claim to represent. I start with the first theme, namely who ISIS says their so-called leaders are:

> The official spokesman of the Khilafah, Shaykh Abu Muhammad al-'Adnani... said, "Rest assured, O soldiers of the Islamic State, for we – by Allah's permission – will carry on upon the manhaj of the imam Shaykh Usamah, the amir of the istishhadiyin[4] Abu Mus'ab az-Zarqawi, the founder of the State Abu 'Umar al-Baghdadi, and its war minister Abu Hamzah al-Muhajir. We will never alter nor change until we taste what they tasted."[5] ... "And when Amirul-Mu'minin Abu 'Umar al- Baghdadi ... gained shahadah alongside Abu Hamzah al-Muhajir...the Islamic State did not waver, rather its leadership unanimously pledged allegiance to Amirul-Mu'minin Abu Bakr al-Baghdadi..."[6]

Here it is clear that ISIS follows the five above-mentioned leaders: Usama Bin Laden, Abu Mus'ab al-Zarqawi, Abu Umar al-Baghdadi, Abu Hamza al-Muhajir, and Abu Bakr al-Baghdadi. A comparison of the life of Prophet Muhammad ﷺ with the actions of the above-mentioned sectarian leaders is an insult to the stature of our Messenger ﷺ and no sane mind can claim that these five leaders were on the Prophetic Methodology. It is enough to mention that the Prophetic Methodology prohibits the killing of civilians, which none of the above-mentioned can claim to have followed. I would also like to emphasize that ISIS, in making Usama Bin Laden its leader, has weakened itself as Bin Laden's AQ organization has been fighting against ISIS since 2013. How can ISIS follow Bin Laden when his followers are killing ISIS' followers? This is a perfect example of the confused minds in ISIS. The next theme to pay attention to is what the ISIS worldview is:

[A]l-Baghdadi: "O Ummah of Islam, indeed the world today has been divided into two camps and two trenches, with no third camp present: The camp of Islam and faith, and the camp of kufr (disbelief) and hypocrisy – the camp of the Muslims and the mujahidin everywhere, and the camp of the jews [*sic*], the crusaders, their allies, and with them the rest of the nations and religions of kufr, all being led by America and Russia, and being mobilized by the jews [*sic*]."⁷…"The first priority is to perform hijrah from wherever you are to the Islamic State, from darul-kufr to darul-Islam…"⁸ "The grayzone is critically endangered, rather on the brink of extinction. Its endangerment began with the blessed operations of September 11th, as these operations manifested two camps before the world for mankind to choose between, a camp of Islam – without the body of Khilafah to represent it at the time – and a camp of kufr – the crusader coalition. Or as Shaykh Usamah Ibn Ladin…said, "The world today is divided into two camps. Bush spoke the truth when he said, 'Either you are with us or you are with the terrorists.' Meaning, either you are with the crusade or you are with Islam."⁹ O Muslims, Islam was never for a day the religion of peace. Islam is the religion of war. Your Prophet ﷺ was dispatched with the sword as a mercy to the creation. He was ordered with war until Allah is worshipped alone…"¹⁰

There are two points that deserve emphasis regarding the ISIS worldview. Firstly ISIS' view of "Islam versus the rest" reflect an "us versus them" mentality and not the "right versus wrong" approach of Muslims, and by saying that (former US President) Bush was right, ISIS is effectively following the (neo-conservative) methodology of Bush and certainly not the Prophetic methodology. The Messenger of Allah ﷺ established the first Islamic State of Medina following the covenant of Medina and it included non-Muslims, even Jewish tribes. The Messenger ﷺ also sent his Companions to live in the Christian kingdom in Abyssinia, hence these two examples are sufficient to neutralize the "us versus them" dichotomy of ISIS.

Secondly, the claim that the Prophet ﷺ was sent with the Sword

3

and ordered with war until Allah is worshipped alone is an attempt at corrupting the Prophetic example, as it is clear from the Messenger's ﷺ twenty-three years of invitation to Islam, merely 200 days (less than a year) out of twenty-three years were spent on wars .

The next theme is "ISIS roadmap to Caliphate."

[...]Abu Mus'ab...implemented the strategy and required tactics to achieve the goal of Khilafah without hesitation. In short, he strived to create as much chaos as possible... With chaos, he intended to prevent any taghut [11] regime from ever achieving a degree of stability... To achieve maximum chaos, the Shaykh focused on the most effective weapons in the arsenal of the mujahidin for creating chaos – vehicle bombs, IEDs, and istishhadiyyin. He would order [sic] to carry out nikayah [12] operations dozens of times in a dozen areas daily, targeting and killing sometimes hundreds of apostates from the police forces and Rafidah...In addition to that, he tried to force every apostate group present in Iraq into an all-out war with Ahlus-Sunnah. [13] So he targeted the Iraqi apostate forces (army, police, and intelligence), the Rafidah (Shia markets, temples, and militias), and the Kurdish secularists (Barzani and Talabani partisans)... Thus, by using methods that led to maximum chaos and targeting apostates of all different backgrounds, the mujahidin were able to keep Iraq in constant instability and war, never allowing any apostate group to enjoy a moment of security...The collapse was followed by the mujahidin quickly entering the vacuum left, to announce and establish the Islamic State of Iraq under the leadership of... Abu 'Umar al-Husayni al-Baghdadi... In short, these phases consist of immigrating to a land with a weak central authority to use as a base where a jama'ah [14] can form, recruit members, and train them...then take advantage of the situation by increasing the chaos to a point leading to the complete collapse of the taghut regime in entire areas, a situation some refer to as "tawahhush" ("mayhem"). The next step would be to fill the vacuum by managing the state of affairs to the point of developing into a full-fledged state, and

4

continuing expansion into territory still under control of the taghut. This has always been the roadmap towards Khilafah for the mujahidin.[15]

This evil strategy outlined by ISIS is their true methodology (*manhaj*) and has no connection whatsoever with the noble character of the Prophet Muhammad ﷺ who was sent by Allah as a mercy to the whole of mankind and to all of the worlds. This nefarious, power-hungry mentality reflects a wicked secular ideology where the means justify the ends, and is impermissible in Islam. This, however, is not surprising, as the whole ISIS project is an attempt at hiding political aims under the cover of Islamic ideology in order to mobilize forces for purely secular and material objectives, such as exacting revenge and seizing power, territory, etc.

The fourth theme is to perceive what ISIS views regarding the Muslims. Regarding the killing of Muslims, they say:

> [A]mongst those who are liable to have their blood shed for the sake of this cause are fellow Muslims who testify that la ilaha illallah. However, these Muslims are renegades whom it's permissible to fight, and for no reason other than the fact that they refuse to give bay'ah (allegiance) to one imam or another.[16]... [M]any of those who say ["La ilaha illallah" have fallen into different shades of shirk at all levels, including shirk in tawassul and du'a, shirk in obedience, ruling and legislation, and shirk in love, support and allegiance.[17] ... So until we return to the correct state of Islamic affairs, it's upon us all to work together to eradicate the principle of "free choice,"[18]... [A] person who ignorantly practices any major shirk or totally abandons practice of the religion's other four pillars (prayer, zakah, siyam, and hajj) can never be considered Muslim, and that is because the very basis of Islam is sincerity and submission. So if someone commits major shirk, he is a mushrik. And if he totally abandons practice of the four pillars, he is a kafir.[19]

Regarding the killing of Shiites and Saudis, they say:

> [A]ssaults by the mujahidin of the Islamic State against the filthy Rawafid [the Shiites]...which resulted in the execution

of 1700 Rafidi [Shiite] soldiers.[20]... Draw your swords. Deal with the Rafidah first, wherever you find them, then Al Salul [Saudi Arabia] and their soldiers before the crusaders and their bases. Deal with the Rafidah, Al Salul, and their soldiers.[21]... As for Yemen...[t]he Rafidi Houthis have entered it, but the car bombs have not roasted their skin, nor have the explosive belts and IEDs severed their joints. Is there not in Yemen a person who will take revenge for us from the Houthis? ...The Khalifah Ibrahim...said in his address: "And O soldiers of Yemen...be harsh against the Houthi Rafidah, for they are kuffar murtaddin. Fight them and overcome them."[22] ... The ruling of apostasy on the Rafidah does not mean they had ever been Muslims [sic] but rather, that they are dealt with much more severely, as they must either enter into Islam or face the sword, as opposed to being treated like kuffar asliyyin[23] who can sometimes be allowed to remain upon their kufr in certain circumstances (treaties, slavery, etc.)[24]

Regarding those whom they consider apostates or idol-worshippers, they say:

The murtadd Hamza Yusuf condemned the attack on Charlie Hebdo[25]... The apostatizing [sic] hypocritical factions are those who moved from the grayzone to the camp of kufr by aiding the blatant murtaddin – the secularist and democratic factions...[26]...Sahwah factions of apostasy kill the people of Islam (the muhajirin and ansar of the Islamic State whom they label Khawarij) and leave the people of idolatry alone (the murtaddin of the Syrian National Coalition and Syrian Interim Government whom they call brothers...[27]... [W]hen the apostates (the Tawaghit and the Rafidah) fight each other, it is not permissible for the Muslim to support one party of apostates against the other...So it is not permissible for the Muslim to fight against Al Salul under the leadership of the Rafidi Houthis nor is it permissible to fight against the Rafidi Houthis under the leadership of Al Salul. If he does fight under the leadership of the taghut in defense of his kufri regime, he apostatizes [*sic*] from Islam.[28]... [T]he apostate Ba'th regime of the taghut Saddam ...the taghut Erdogan regime ... the tawaghit of Turkey, Al Salul, and Qatar — the triad of apostasy — mobilized without seeking permission from their crusader masters. They gained support from the Arab and non-Arab tawaghit of Bahrain, Kuwait, the UAE, Egypt, Jordan, Morocco, Senegal, Bangladesh, Sudan, Pakistan, and Somalia, to aid the taghut regime of Abd Rabbuh Mansur Hadi against the Rafidah of the Houthis and Ali Abdullah Saleh in Yemen. ...The apostate triad — Turkey, Al Salul, and Qatar — also funneled aid to a newly formed coalition of factions addicted to taghut support — "Jaysh al-Fath"[29]

The order of the ISIS "Caliph":

This is the order of the Khalifah...Either ones [*sic*] performs hijrah to the wilayat of the Khilafah or, if he is unable to do so, he must attack the crusaders, their allies, the Rafidah, the tawaghit, and their apostate forces, wherever he might be with any means available to him, and he should not hesitate in doing so, nor consult any supposed "scholar" on this obligation. He should attack after declaring his bay'ah to the Khilafah, so as not to die a death of Jahiliyyah.[30]

In order to simplify the above-mentioned quotes about ISIS' views regarding Muslims, it suffices to emphasize that in its eyes the only real Muslims are those who are ISIS-affiliated; Muslims who do not become a part of them are one of following categories: [apostates (*murtaddun*), disbelievers (*kuffar*), idolaters (*tawaghit*), rejectionist Shiites (*Rafida*), or polytheists (*mushrikun*), supported by crusaders, Jews, heretics, etc.]

Hence, having merely cited direct quotes from ISIS in relation to their terrorist leaders, their binary worldview, their strategic roadmap of chaos, and their views toward other Muslims, we see clearly that they are not upholding the Prophetic methodology. They even treat non-Muslims (including Yazidi slaves) better than Muslims who don't become a part of them.

CHAPTER II

Proving that the Followers of ISIS are Khawarij

DESPITE THE FACT that the members of ISIS (Islamic State of Iraq and Syria) are nominally Muslims, they have in fact left Sunni Islam due to the beliefs they hold and the horrid crimes they have deemed permissible in contradiction to Islamic law. One can say that they are close to leaving Islam entirely and have certainly morphed into another faction, oscillating between belief and disbelief, though closer to disbelief. For this reason, describing them as Sunni is incorrect.

Furthermore, describing them as Muslims is a matter of speculation and a point of contention, as we shall see in this fatwa. That is because they have committed three heinous acts: (1) revolting against the Muslim community, rulers, as well as the public (2) anathematizing the majority of Sunni Muslims, and (3) considering the spread of injustice and corruption across the land by killing, wanton destruction, and plundering as permissible.

These crimes in particular bring to mind the strong parallel between ISIS and the Khawarij of the early days of Islam, who adopted extremist tendencies and anathematized any Muslim—including many illustrious Companions of the Prophet ﷺ—who did not adopt their beliefs, They took advantage of the political instability at the time, culminating in a revolt against the Caliph 'Ali ؓ which precipitated much chaos and loss of life before their movement was quelled.

The Prophet Muhammad ﷺ foretold the advent of the Khawarij, and despite their outward adherence to religion, he described them, as found in the two rigorously authentic hadith collections of al-Bukhari and Muslim, as "the worst of mankind and animals."[31] He ﷺ also mentioned that "they shall pass out of the religion just as an arrow passes out of the prey"[32]—referring to the ease and definitiveness with which they exit the fold of Islam. In reference to the facade of their overt religiosity, the Prophet 🕊 said "they shall call to the Book of Allah though they do not belong to it."[33]

Their wretched standing in the eyes of Allah Almighty is clear, as the Prophet 🕊 said they are "the worst of those who are killed under the sky"[34]; and "glad tidings to the one who kills them and the one whom they kill."[35] He 🕊 also described them as "the dogs of Hell"[36] and that "they seek the extremities of the religion until they leave it."[37] As narrated in *Sahih Muslim*, the Prophet 🕊 stated that "they are the creation most hated by Allah Most-High"[38]—which would imply that their status is worse than even that of disbelievers.

Likewise, he 🕊 prophesied, as related in the two rigorously authentic collections of al-Bukhari and Muslim from 'Ali 🕊, that that "There shall emerge a people in the end of time, adolescent, dim-witted, recounting the best words of creation, reading the Quran, but their faith does not pass their throats. They shall pass out of the religion just as an arrow passes out of the prey. So wherever you meet them, kill them for truly in killing them is a great reward with Allah on the Day of Judgement."[939] (It is important to note that these narrations are not an endorsement for vigilante action, as the assumption is that fighting them is conducted under proper authority.)

The words of the Prophet 🕊, "There shall emerge a people in the end of time," refer to the followers of ISIS and point to them being intended, not only the group which already emerged during the Caliphate of 'Ali 🕊. Other evidences alluding to the Khawarij manifesting through numerous eras include the words of the Prophet 🕊, "Whenever a generation of theirs emerges, Allah Almighty severs it." The narrator of this tradition said, "The Messenger 🕊 repeated that twenty or more times while I listened," and in one variant, "until the last one of them emerges with the Anti-Christ."[40]

9

CHAPTER III

ISIS' Atrocities

THERE HAVE BEEN numerous reports of the dreadful crimes and slaughter perpetrated by those affiliated with ISIS against men and women, young and old, Muslims and non-Muslims alike. It seems that there are few types of crimes that ISIS has not committed. Their transgressions can be summed up in the following categories:

Indiscriminate Killing & Brutality
1. Killing the innocent based on unsubstantiated evidence, inconsistent claims, fabricated accusations, and hasty prosecutions, all of which places the blood of thousands of innocent people on their hands, for which they will be questioned on the Day of Judgement.
2. Killing foreigners under treaty or those who have entered our lands under the security of the Muslims, for no sin other than belonging to specific nationalities. ISIS did not take into account that they were either aid workers or journalists working to report on the suffering inside Syria to the world. This is one of the ugliest forms of deception, as I shall explain. Examples of this include the ruthless beheading of American journalist, James Foley.[41]
3. Exacting revenge upon the public in areas which ISIS took control of, especially the children of Syrian and Iraqi families. The Sha'itat tribe in the Deir ez-Zor province is one of the most salient examples of this, where ISIS massacred over 700 members of the tribe in August 2014 for simply resisting ISIS' takeover of their land.[42]
4. Kidnapping foreigners and killing those who embraced Islam after being kidnapped. Killing a prisoner after he embraces Islam is impermissible; he must either be freed or pay a ransom. This is

the tragic case of the American aid worker Abdur Rahman Kassig who was executed by ISIS.[43]

5. Burning Muslims alive[44] as in the case of the Jordanian pilot Muath al-Kasasbeh, which is decisively impermissible. The analogy between burning and bombing which ISIS attempts to employ, using the claim of retributive justice, is categorically false. Firstly, it is obligatory to proceed with caution in matters of life and death, as "to err in pardoning is better than to err in punishing." Secondly, retributive justice is restricted to that which is permitted by the Shariah, and al-Bukhari narrates in his *Sahih* collection that the Messenger of Allah ﷺ forbade torture with fire. The ultimate aims of Shariah are based on preventing injustice. In the words of Allah Almighty, ❨*If you punish, then punish with the like of that wherewith you were afflicted*❩ (16:126). Hence, there is a command to the believers not to exceed the bounds of what is necessary when redressing transgressions. Retributive justice is legal in the fighting itself, not with respect to how it is implemented, and therefore, in doing so, one is only allowed to employ the means permitted by the Shariah.

6. Killing a number of scholars, imams, and Friday speakers in Syria and Iraq for no reason other than their adherence to classical Sunni doctrine as represented by the Ash'ari and Maturidi theological schools. They do not differentiate between Sufis and Salafis in their anathematization, and they accuse the people of Sufism (Islamic spirituality) who adhere to the four Sunni schools of law to be outside the pale of Islam.[45]

7. Torturing prisoners resulting in their death, humiliating prisoners in front of audiences, and killing the injured during battle, all of which are strictly prohibited in Islam.[46]

8. Committing torture by using knives and blades or random gunfire upon groups of prisoners, as well as terrorizing individuals with repeated threats of death. All of this is impermissible in Islam. The Prophet ﷺ commanded us to kill in an ethical manner, as he said, "Truly Allah prescribed perfection upon everything; so if you kill then kill properly." The meaning of this is that if a man must kill with just cause, he should choose the means which is most merciful to the culprit. As for killing the innocent,

mutilating their bodies, decapitating them while filming it all, the law of Allah has not permitted this for criminals or even enemies, let alone the innocent and helpless.

9. Mutilating corpses and disrespecting the bodies of the dead.[47] This is impermissible in Islam, even for one's sworn enemies, due to the hadith, "cutting the bones of the deceased is like cutting his bones while alive." The deceased feels the pain felt by the living, as his sanctity is akin to the sanctity of the living. The Prophet ﷺ prohibited mutilation. Treating the heads of the deceased as prizes is amongst the most degrading forms of mutilation. Likewise, leaving the deceased without proper burial is impermissible in Islam.

Belittling the Sacred Law

10. Appointing fanatics and ignorant people as judges, who have neither experience nor any knowledge of jurisprudence to pass judgement in the name of Islam regarding the blood and wealth of people. This is one of the greatest disasters brought on by this group, since they are repelling the public from the Shariah despite it being full of mercy, justice, and wisdom. Ibn Qayyim al-Jawziyya said regarding the Shariah, "The bedrock and foundation of the Shariah is wisdom and benefit for people in this life and the next. It is all justice, mercy, benefit, and wisdom. Every ruling that leaves justice for injustice, that leaves mercy for its opposite, that leaves benefit for corruption, that leaves wisdom for folly, is not from the Shariah, even if it is inserted through interpretation."

[It is incorrect for a neophyte or an amateur student of knowledge who has read a few books or articles on his own to assume the weighty responsibility of passing legal judgements, let alone a complete ignoramus to assume a position of authority and pass judgements that lead to the implementation of execution, stoning, or whipping. Even a doctorate in Shariah does not produce a judge, just as reading a book regarding the jurisprudence of the Sunna does not produce a jurist. Judgement, as the scholars have noted, is a precise skill which is not possessed by every jurist. The method of implementing rulings according to context and actual events is not acquired through books, but rather by accompanying the

12

judges or muftis and studying the nuances of giving legal verdicts.

Al-Tusuli mentions in his commentary on *Tuhfat al-Hukkam*, "The science of judgement may be from the branches of jurisprudence but it differs by matters that not every jurist will master. Perhaps one of the people is well-versed in the chapter of disputes but has no expertise in other than that. It is not difficult to distinguish the science of judgement from other branches of jurisprudence, but the difficulty is in using and implementing the general principles of jurisprudence on the minutia of actual events. That is difficult. You may find a man who has memorised much of knowledge and teaches others, but when questioned by the public about an incident relating to oaths or something similar, he is not able to properly respond."

11. Implementing the capital punishments[48] at a time when they should be suspended, such as during war, famine, poverty, and a general state of ignorance. I authored a book entitled, *The Ruling of Implementing the Capital Punishments*, in which I elaborated on the hindrances to applying capital punishments. I relied upon evidences from the Sunna, the actions of the Companions, the four Sunni schools of law, and the words of the jurists. In this work, I proved that the ruler has the right, and sometimes the obligation, to suspend implementation of the penal code when extenuating circumstances are present.

12. Expelling Muslims and non-Muslims from their towns and villages[49], illegally seizing properties, and terrorizing the innocent for merely rejecting their views and detesting their crimes.

Destruction of Sites

13. Destroying mosques, pillaging graves, and dishonoring the sanctity of Allah and the sanctity of the living. ISIS has been responsible for the razing of many mosques and tombs, most notably, those of the Prophet Jonah[50] ﷺ and the Prophet Daniel[51] ﷺ in Mosul, Iraq. The irreverence of this group does not spare even the Prophets of Allah All-Mighty, the greatest and most honored of creation, further demonstrating its extremism and blatant blasphemy. In addition, ISIS has been responsible for the

destruction of several other mosques, such as the Hamou Qadu mosque in Mosul, a historic structure dating back to the Ottoman period. ISIS provides as justification the claim that these sacred places contain symbols of idolatry and innovation. It should be noted that Muslims have never believed that erecting mausoleums for the Prophets and saints equates to apportioning divinity to them; hence, this group's destruction of the houses of God are heinous crimes based on faulty reasoning and a primitive understanding of Islamic monotheism. Allah All-Mighty says in the Quran, ❮And who are more unjust than those who prevent the name of Allah from being mentioned in His mosques and strive toward their destruction?❯ (2:114)

14. Destroying churches and other houses of worship. The Shariah has obligated Islamic leadership to protect churches, synagogues, temples, and other houses of worship under its dominion. Allah All-Mighty says, ❮Had it not been that Allah checks one set of people by means of another, monasteries, churches, synagogues, and mosques wherein the name of Allah is oft-mentioned would surely have been demolished.❯ (22:40) Examples abound in Islamic history where the caliph took direct responsibility for the protection of the houses of worship of other faiths. When the Caliph 'Umar entered Jerusalem after the conquest in year 637 CE and the time for prayer had come, he refused to pray in a nearby church, despite being offered to do so by the head priest Sophronius, for fear that the Muslims may interpret the action as a precedent to convert the church to a mosque. Compare this to the actions of ISIS, who have blown up several churches in Syria and Iraq, including the St. Markorkous Church in Mosul[52], one of the oldest in the city.

15. Destroying sites of historical and cultural significance. ISIS is bent on decimating any remnants of culture in the region, notable examples being their demolition of important artefacts from the World Heritage Site in Palmyra[53] and their demolition of the ancient Assyrian city of Nimrud.[54]

Anathemization

16. Anathematizing anyone who calls to democracy[55], without a thorough examination and clarification of what is intended.

This is despite the fact that the majority of Muslims who call for democracy intend by it the principles of justice and consultation, and the right of the people to choose their ruler. It is a principle in the Shariah that if customary meanings are established, they are taken into account in legal rulings and given precedence over linguistic definitions. For example, the majority of rulings in jurisprudence pertaining to oaths are based on customary meanings. It is well known that the customary meaning of democracy as established and understood by the public is consultation and justice. Likewise, this is the meaning a number of Muslim preachers have adopted. The vast majority of those in Muslim lands who call for democracy do not intend rejection of Islamic law or denial of the existence of Allah Almighty. The Muslim masses do not consider anything superior or more beneficial to their lives than the law of Allah Almighty. Therefore, the attempts of ISIS to excommunicate the vast majority of Muslims on the grounds of their desire for democratically elected governments are completely baseless.

17. Considering themselves the only saved group of Muslims, that they are an Islamic state, and that anybody opposing them is an apostate who must be fought and killed.[56] I shall elaborate on this point in the next chapter.

Enslavement

18. Enslaving non-Muslims.[57] The jurists in recent times have unanimously agreed that slavery is invalid and impermissible, except in the case where the enemy enslaves our women, which has clearly not occurred. The impermissibility of slavery in Islam has been established as a result of Muslims adhering to international agreements of mutual benefit for humanity. This agreement banning slavery resembles the League of the Virtuous (*ḥilf al-fuḍūl*) which was a pact entered by the Prophet ﷺ prior to Islam, the purpose of which was to prevent injustice and oppression, to take retribution against criminals, and to aid the weak and oppressed. After the advent of Islam, the Prophet ﷺ commented that had he been invited to this same league now, he would have surely responded to the call.

15

These international agreements stipulate the impermissibility of slavery, which does not contradict the Shariah, the Sunna, or the Quran. A Muslim ruler is entitled to enter a treaty with non-Muslims that neither shall enslave any prisoners of war, and Muslims are bound to that covenant. Eradicating slavery through such agreements does not nullify the rulings of slavery in Islam as transmitted through the Quran and Sunna, but rather such an arrangement is based upon acting equitably in the best interests of humanity. If other nations were to break their contracts and begin enslaving Muslims or non-Muslim citizens in Muslim nations, then it would be permissible for the Muslims to retaliate accordingly against the violating nations.

The enslaving of Yazidi men, women, and children by ISIS[58] is a tragedy and a major violation of global human rights agreements. Muslims must be the first to condemn this as they are obligated by Allah to stand by their contracts. Allah Almighty says in the Quran, ❴O you who believe! Fulfil all contracts.❵ (5:1). Regardless of the difference of opinion surrounding the classification of the Yazidis as People of the Book, enslaving them is completely unsupported by the principles of the Shariah. Even if ISIS was to implement the principle of retributive justice, the Yazidis have not enslaved any Muslims to warrant such retaliatory measures. They are a peaceful people with whom Muslims have lived side-by-side in harmony for centuries.

19. Raping women[59] and kidnapping children[60] using various pretexts with which they pervert the religion. They select the opinions that concur with their sick desires, such as claiming "possessions of the right hand" or claiming the necessity of jihad. Despite there being no justification for the kidnapping of children, they have turned many young boys into criminals and forcibly separated them from their families to train them for jihad.

Harming Islam

20. Harming Islam and Muslims around the world and distorting the image of the prophetic message. Allah Almighty said regarding the Seal of all Prophets ﷺ, ❴We sent you not, but as a mercy to the worlds.❵ (21:107) ISIS is not concerned with harm befalling

Muslims across the world as a result of their actions, nor are they concerned about people turning away from Islam.

ISIS affirms, confesses, and exults in all of the aforementioned crimes and transgressions in front of the world's media and other spectators. There is hardly a place under its control that is void of unjustly slaughtered victims and innocent prisoners. The followers of ISIS do not care about the sanctity of human life, pacts of peace with non-Muslims, nor the bond of fraternity with Muslims.

All of these transgressions bring forth the obligation to fight this group in order to shatter its forces, stop its crimes, and rid mankind of its evil.

CHAPTER IV

ISIS' Anathematizing Muslims from Islam

ONE OF THE biggest enormities committed by ISIS is their anathem-ization of Muslims[61]; not simply an individual or a small group but rather the entire Muslim nation.[62] They only consider themselves to be true followers of Islam, and have already anathematized anyone who fights them and anathematized the Muslim rulers and anyone who give allegiance to these rulers.[63] In fact, they deem anyone who opposes them to be a disbeliever.[64] Despite the fact that they claim to be Salafis, they anathematize the majority of Salafis, and despite the fact that they call for jihad, they are the ghastliest enemy of the Mujahidun.

They support their anathematization and murder through invalid evidences and clear logical fallacies. They are, as Ibn 'Umar described, those who "rushed to the verses regarding the disbelievers and applied them to the believers"—ignorant of the principles of legal judgement (*ijtihad*) and devoid of all knowledge and skill required by a *mujtahid* (one who legitimately exercises *ijtihad*). Therefore, their interpretation is disregarded and their opinions are ignored as they select revealed texts stripped of context that agree with their desires, reject all others, and accept neither the fatwa of a rightly-guided scholar nor the judgement of a true judge.

In the opinion of a number of scholars, they have already left Islam due to their aberrant beliefs. No one should be deceived by the prayers and fasts they perform. The Prophet ﷺ clarified this, as he said in a tradition transmitted by al-Bukhari and Muslim and narrated by Abu Sa'id al-Khudri ﷺ regarding their description, "You shall belittle your prayer and fasting alongside their prayer and fasting." We should not be deceived by their disingenuous call to rule by the law of Allah Almighty. They truly are as 'Ali ﷺ described, "Calling to truth though they are not on it." All of the killing, torture, destruction of mosques, desecration of graves, expulsion of people, and looting of wealth are the furthest possible actions from Sharia rulings, Prophetic morals and the tolerance of Islam.

Many individuals have defected from ISIS and have revealed its beliefs as well as the reality of its treatment of any opposition. One of the strongest testimonies for this is what *Asharq Al-Awsat* reported from a Tunisian who defected from ISIS, saying, "If you don't work with ISIS and profess allegiance to it then you are ignorant of the religion and you should be killed even if you are unaware of the gravity of your position. A second point, if a scholar declared that it is permissible to not take retribution against an ignorant person due to his ignorance—i.e., by presenting an excuse for him— then the likes of this scholar is, according to ISIS' literature, a disbeliever who should also be killed."

It is enough of a proof of the extreme ideology of ISIS that the top leaders of Salafi-Jihadism have disclaimed it.[65] The best statement that applies to them is the hadith of the Prophet ﷺ, "Beware of saying to your brother 'disbeliever' (*kafir*) because it will apply to one of you. If it is, he will be it and if it is not, it returns to you." Ibn 'Abd al-Barr says in his book *al-Istidhkar*, "The meaning of 'it returns' is that he bears the burden of its sin."

Anathematizing the Muslims plays a crucial role in ISIS' ideology, as they use the claim of apostasy to judge the blood of Muslims lawful to spill, thereby providing justification for the wars they conduct,[66] disguising their lust for power under the cloak of religious concern.

CHAPTER V

Are the Khawarij Muslims?

THE OPINION OF the majority of traditional jurists regarding the infamous Khawarij is that it is a legal obligation to fight them, without deeming them disbelievers. They would consider them misguided and disobedient to Allah Almighty and to His Messenger 鑫.

Abu Bakr al-Ajurri said, "None of the scholars, in either past or recent times, ever disagreed that the Khawarij are an evil group, disobedient to Allah Almighty and to His Messenger 鑫. Even if they pray, fast, or strive in worship, it does not benefit them, and even if they openly enjoin good and forbid evil it does not benefit them, as they are a people who interpret the Quran according to their desire.[67]

I was raised amongst scholars who would not dare hasten in anathematizing anybody, and I constantly repeat my noble father's statement to my students, "To keep a thousand men within the fold of Islam by a slight chance is more beloved to us than to expel a single man from the fold of Islam by suspicion." However, a number of senior jurists in the past and in recent times have unequivocally passed judgement on the disbelief of the Khawarij. Whoever looks at the extremism of the followers of ISIS in their beliefs and sees their audacity in declaring those who oppose them to be disbelievers, their persistence in shedding the blood of innocent Muslims and their deeming unlawful things lawful, would hardly doubt the validity of this ruling and its application to them in this time.

Abu Bakr Ibn al-'Arabi adopted this opinion and said:

The correct opinion is that they are disbelievers due to the words of the Prophet 鑫, "They shall pass out of the religion," and his words, "I shall truly kill them as 'Ad were killed." In another narration the nation of Thamud is mentioned, both of whom perished due to disbelief. Likewise, his words, "They are the worst of creation," which are not ascribed to any except disbelievers, and his words, "Truly they are the most hated of creation by Allah Almighty." Furthermore, due to their passing the judgement of disbelief on all who oppose them and declaring their eternal damnation in Hell, they (Khawarij) are far more deserving of this name than them.[68]

Imam al-Qurtubi al-Maliki inclined to this opinion, as he said when commenting on the prophetic saying, "They shall pass out of the religion...":

The meaning of this simile is that this group shall leave the religion of Islam without having any association with it." Hence, our scholars have clung to the apparent meaning of this simile in declaring them disbelievers. Many scholars hesitated in declaring them disbelievers because of his ﷺ words, "there is quarrelling regarding the nock," implying doubt regarding them. However, it seems that the first opinion, the opinion that they are already disbelievers, is more evident from the hadith.[69]

Shaykh 'Abd al-'Aziz Ibn Baz issued a fatwa in which he declared the Khawarij disbelievers, saying, "The majority are of the opinion that they are disobedient misguided innovators, though they do not deem them disbelievers. However, the correct opinion is that they are disbelievers."[70]

CHAPTER VI

The Obligation to Advise
Them Prior to Fighting

IT IS IMPERMISSIBLE to begin fighting the Khawarij before presenting them with advice, clarifying their positions of error, and explaining uncertainties. In our letter to their leader, I and other Muslim scholars advised them, clarified their errors, directed them to that which is right, and warned them of the error they shall fall into, but they did not take heed.[71]

For this reason, after they have spilt innocent blood, after they have received advice and clarification, despite their ongoing persistence and oppression, fighting them has become an obligation for Muslims.

The legal ruling in Islam is that the Khawarij should not be fought except after two things:

1. *Advice is given to them and the truth is clarified.* This is what 'Ali ﷺ did with the Khawarij of his time when he sent 'Abdullah Ibn 'Abbas ﷺ to debate them and clarify matters for them. Four thousand individuals repented and returned with him.[72] Additionally, al-Bukhari included a chapter in the section "Asking Apostates and Rebels to Repent and Fighting Them," entitled "Fighting the Khawarij after Establishing Proof against Them."[73] Ibn Battal said in his commentary on *Sahih al-Bukhari*: "It means that fighting a kharijite or others is not obligatory except after calling him to the truth and explaining what is unclear for him so that no excuse is left. If he then refuses to turn back to the truth, fighting him becomes obligatory. The evidence for this is from the words of Allah Almighty, ❨*And Allah will not mislead a people*

after He hath guided them, until after He made clear to them what to fear.
(9:115) We must adhere to the example that Allah Almighty has set forth regarding the people we have to fight by clarifying the truth to them and calling them to it."[74]

2. *They transgress and kill.* As long as they remain peaceful and do not expose anyone to harm they are left as they are. However, when they unlawfully spill blood or take to brigandage, fighting them becomes obligatory for the leader.

Imam Ahmad relates a saying of 'Abdullah b. Shaddad regarding 'Ali ﷺ and the Khawarij, "The contract between us and you is that you shall not spill blood unlawfully, take to brigandage, or oppress non-Muslim citizens. Indeed, if you do that, then we shall declare war against you accordingly. Verily Allah loves not the treacherous." 'A'isha ﷺ then said, "O Ibn Shaddad, he killed them!" He responded, "By Allah, he did not send an army to them until they took to brigandage, spilt blood, and deemed killing non-Muslim citizens permissible"[75]—meaning that he did not send an army to fight them until they committed these crimes. Look at his words, "Until they deemed killing non-Muslim citizens permissible," to know the obligation upon Muslims in protecting non-Muslims who live with them when some Muslims transgress against them.

Abu 'Ubayd al-Qasim b. Sallam related on the authority of Abu Mijlaz that "'Ali forbade his companions from stretching out their hands [in fighting] the Khawarij until they committed a crime."[76] The meaning of this is that he forbade them from fighting them until they committed a grave crime.

CHAPTER VII

Fighting ISIS is Obligatory

Allah Almighty says in the Holy Quran, ❨*Hence, if two groups of believers fall to fighting, reconcile between them; but then, if one of the two groups transgresses against the other, fight against the one that transgressed until it reverts to the commandment of Allah; and if it does, reconcile again between them with justice, and deal equitably with them: for verily, Allah loves those who act equitably!*❩ (49:9)

The Prophet ﷺ commanded fighting the Khawarij without hesitation in order to eradicate the fear and oppression that spreads throughout society at their hands. He said in a narration transmitted by al-Bukhari and Muslim, "If I encounter them I shall truly kill them like 'Ad was killed."[77] He also commanded pursuing them to kill them, as related in the two *Sahih* collections from the narration of 'Ali, "Wherever you encounter them, kill them, for truly in killing them is a reward on the Day of Judgement for whoever does so."[78]

The Prophet ﷺ expounded upon the reward for the one who kills them and the reward for those killed by them, and informed us of their emergence and rebellion in numerous eras, as he ﷺ said, narrated by Imam Ahmad, "When they emerge, kill them, then when they emerge again, kill them, then when they emerge again, kill them. Glad tidings to whoever kills them and whomever they kill."[79]

In light of these proofs from the Prophetic traditions, Muslim Scholars in the past and in recent times passed judgement on the obligation of fighting the Khawarij. Ibn Taymiyya said, "The predecessors of the Muslim Nation and their imams agreed upon fighting them."[80] Ibn Hubayra said, "Indeed fighting the Khawarij is more necessary than fighting the polytheists, for in fighting them there is preservation of the core of Islam."[81]

For this reason, I issue the fatwa that fighting the group known as ISIS is a *communal obligation* (*fard kifayya*) upon Muslims. This group must be fought in order to protect the core of the religion, defend Muslim lands, protect the blood of the innocent, and raise the banner of truth. It is not permissible to neglect fighting ISIS and whoever neglects fighting it, from those upon whom fighting is mandatory, is sinful. If Muslims do not stand to repel the evil of this treacherous faction, they will all be sinful. Furthermore, the burden of guilt on the rulers is heavier, as jihad can only be conducted under the command of a legitimate ruler.

Any Muslim who embarks on war against ISIS is truly a *mujahid* in the way of Allah Almighty, obedient to Him, establishing an obligation of the religion, and acting on behalf of all Muslims. Whoever is killed in this war at the hands of ISIS is not simply a martyr, but rather the best martyr, just as the Prophet 鷺 mentioned.[82]

A Call to the Followers of ISIS to Repent

Along with this fatwa on the obligation of fighting these Khawarij, I make a final appeal to their followers, men and women. I call upon them to retreat, repent to Allah Almighty, and return to their roots, Sunni Islam. It is impermissible to waste the abilities of the Muslim youth with a war that is destroying Islam, harming it, distorting its image, chasing people away from it, and provoking hatred and extremism against Muslims. It is a war for the sake of a man who is bartering with Islam to quench his thirst for blood and satisfy his hunger for power.

CHAPTER VIII

The Invalidity of the Oath of Allegiance to al-Baghdadi

ALLAH ALMIGHTY DESCRIBES the believers as ❨*those whose rule is done by consultation amongst themselves*❩ (42:38), referring to government, supreme authority, the grand Caliphate, and the election of a legitimate ruler. Al-Bukhari narrates in his *Sahih* collection that 'Umar ﷺ said, "Whoever swears allegiance to a man without consulting the Muslims is not to be given allegiance to, nor the one whom he gave allegiance to, in fear they both may be killed."[83]

The Caliphate is a public affair linked to the entire Muslim Nation and cannot be settled by a few juveniles, nor can the foolish engage in discussing it. Dignitaries who exert authority within the Muslim Nation are the ones who have sole right to it. And these dignitaries already chose a king, emir, sultan, or president for their countries, responsible for their economic and political affairs. Therefore, allegiance to the leader of ISIS known as Abu Bakr al-Baghdadi is fundamentally impermissible and ultimately void, bearing no legal consequence as the local Muslim authorities were not consulted, neither in Syria nor in Iraq.

Despite al-Baghdadi's claims to the position of caliph, it is evident that he is far from qualified for this weighty position. Testimony against him, stating his deviance and incompetence, comes from none other than one of his teachers, Abu 'Abdillah Muhammad al-Mansur (al-'Isawi), the commander of what is called "The Mujahidin Army in Iraq," and one of the top leaders of the Salafi-Jihadi movement. I quote him as a further proof against al-Baghdadi, because al-Baghdadi was his former student, who gave him allegiance and then subsequently defected to form his own group. Al-Mansur authored a book refuting the falsehood of ISIS, entitled "The Islamic State between Reality and Illusion," where he describes this self-proclaimed caliph as being villainous, ignorant, and deviant. He also says, "He did not master one single book in theology or jurisprudence"—further validating that this group does not operate based on any Islamic understanding or principles. It is telling that, even to a jihadi leader, al-Baghdadi's extremism and ignorance are unrivalled. The list of leaders of the Salafi-Jihadi movement who attacked ISIS and its leadership and opposed its systematic policy of anathematization, murder, and brutality is almost endless.[84] In addition, there are numerous examples of his own followers who abandoned him, disparaged him, and rejected his claim to the caliphate.

Therefore, the one who gives allegiance to al-Baghdadi is neither required to uphold the oath nor obey the one given allegiance. Maintaining allegiance to him is a major sin and a cause of schism in the community.

I call on the brigades in Syria who have given allegiance to ISIS to defect, as it is impermissible to assist these misguided criminals in killing the innocent and distorting the image of Islam. Defecting from ISIS is indeed a religious obligation. It is not treacherous to abandon al-Baghdadi, but rather the real treachery for Muslims is swearing allegiance to the leader of a group that tortures Muslims and deems their masses as disbelievers.

It must be pointed out that obedience to the leaders and commanders of this group is legally impermissible as one cannot obey a created being in disobedience to the Creator, especially if the matter is related to murder, torture, and harassment. It is obligatory upon one who can flee and save himself to do so immediately, lest he become responsible for innocent blood on the Day of Judgement.

CHAPTER IX

Seeking Assistance from Non-Muslims

ISIS HAS BASED their anathematization of rulers and the population at large primarily on the notion that seeking help from non-Muslims means agreeing to their beliefs. With this in mind, I thought it important to shed some light on the legal ruling of seeking help from non-Muslims in times of war, concluding that it is permissible. Furthermore, if it is permissible in times of war, then its permissibility in times of peace is greater, thereby nullifying a fundamental principle that ISIS has used to spill the blood of innocent Muslims.

The majority of jurists were of the opinion that it is permissible for Muslims, when fighting the Khawarij, to seek assistance from non-Muslims in times of necessity, whether that be through additional fighters, weapons, or experience, if the Muslims are lacking. Leaning on such assistance is not considered supporting a non-Muslim against a Muslim, but rather it is supporting Islam, establishing the religion, and eradicating corruption from the Earth.

ISIS justifies its stance using the hadith of 'A'isha ﷺ, recorded in *Sahih Muslim*, in which the Prophet ﷺ sent back a polytheist who came to fight with the Muslims after asking him, "Do you believe in Allah and His Messenger?" The man said, "No." The Prophet ﷺ then said, "Return, for I shall never seek help from a polytheist."[85] This hadith is understood in the context that either there was no necessity in seeking the polytheist's services, or the Prophet ﷺ instructed him to return in hope that he would embrace Islam—which he did, as is mentioned in the end of the hadith.

Al-Nawawi said:

It has been reported in another hadith that the Prophet ﷺ sought help from Safwan b. Umayya before he embraced Islam. So a group of scholars took the first narration as a general overruling statement, whereas Imam al-Shafi'i and others [took the opinion] that if the non-Muslim provides only advice to Muslims and necessity calls for seeking his help, his help could be sought, and if there is no need then it is disliked. Hence, by applying the two requirements, he put both narrations in effect.[86]

In fact, the scholars used this opinion to pass judgement during the war to liberate Kuwait.[87]

Seeking assistance from non-Muslims today is to strengthen the true vision of Islam that the Prophet ﷺ was sent with and to eradicate the evil of this rebellious group. Islam is truly a religion of mercy, wisdom, justice, tolerance and peace. Muslims have been known throughout history for observing covenants, even when the covenants harmed them, and that was one of the most significant reasons for the spread of Islam.

The actions of ISIS are corrosive, distorting the image of Islam, harming it, and chasing people away from the religion. In actuality, ISIS is doing a great service to those who hate Islam, as they think this perversion is in fact Islam.

When we seek assistance from non-Muslims we do so to support Muslims across the world, from Indonesia to Morocco, as ISIS has supporters in every country. If they were able, they would commit the same heinous acts or worse in other countries.[88]

This seeking of assistance is not tantamount to agreeing with non-Muslims on their beliefs, but rather it is the exchanging of mutual benefit. They have an evident interest which does not contradict Islam, and that is to protect their lives and their lands from these Khawarij who revolted, broke covenants, killed non-Muslims citizens, and incited people in countries with whom we have covenants to act treacherously and violate their contracts. The Prophet ﷺ said, in a narration recorded by al-Bukhari and Muslim, "A banner shall be raised for every traitor on the Day of Judgement saying 'This is the treachery of so-and-so.'"[89]

[handwritten margin note: Saudi mention of cooperation with non-Muslims.]

In fact, the benefits for Muslims in this are greater and more important than they are for non-Muslims.

Shaykh 'Abd al-'Aziz Ibn Baz said, when explaining the difference between seeking assistance and agreement with non-Muslim beliefs:

> Some people think that seeking assistance from polytheists is considered agreement with their beliefs. It is not, as seeking assistance is one thing and agreement with their beliefs is another. The Prophet 🙴, when seeking assistance from al-Mut'im b. 'Addi, 'Abdullah ibn Urayqit, or the Jews of Khaybar, was not agreeing with the polytheists' beliefs or giving them authority over Muslims. Rather, he did that out of need for them, to utilise them in matters that would benefit the Muslims and not harm them. Likewise, his sending the emigrants from Mecca to Abyssinia was not an agreement with the beliefs of the Christians, but rather he did that in the interests of the Muslims, to mitigate harms coming to them. Therefore, it is incumbent on Muslims to distinguish between that which Allah distinguishes and to utilize each proof in its proper place—and Allah is the Giver of success.[90]

The author of the abovementioned fatwa, Shaykh 'Abd al-'Aziz Ibn Baz, was the previous mufti of Saudi Arabia, the Chairman of the Permanent Committee for Islamic Research and Fatwa, and the President of the "Supreme Council of Scholars (Saudi Arabia)." He was a pivotal figure in the modern Salafi movement. (I use this name Salafi with reservations to avoid its monopoly by a single group, as the majority of Sunni Muslims follow the scholars of the pious predecessors—the *Salaf*—like Imams Abu Hanifa, Malik, al-Shafi'i, and Ahmad.)

CHAPTER X

Legal Rulings Regarding Muslims in Western Countries

MUSLIMS WHO LIVE in non-Muslim lands in any continent, whether the population consists of People of the Book like the United States of America, or consist of other faiths like in China and Japan, have entered those countries under covenant and contract, manifested in either the visa, documents for residency, or citizenship. Each of these documents which are obtained by a Muslim in non-Muslim lands contain an agreement, signature, and consent that he or she is a peaceful resident, not a combatant, or that he or she is a citizen and shall protect the land in which he or she is staying, not be an enemy of it.

Deception and treachery are not permissible for Muslims who live in Western countries, such as the U.S. or Canada, or in the Far East in China or Japan, or anywhere else in the world, such as Brazil, Scandinavia, or Australia. It is impermissible for them to go against their contract. They must respect the law of the lands in which they live, as was the case of the Companions of the Prophet ﷺ when they migrated from Mecca to Abyssinia and lived many years under the shade of a just Christian king. They found security with him despite the fact that his people were Christians who opposed their faith.

'Alā' al-Din al-Haskafi al-Hanafi said, "Any Muslim who enters the land of war under the pledge of security cannot kill, loot, or commit fornication with any one of them, as Muslims stand by their contract."[91] We must note that there is no war between Muslims and Western Countries today. War cannot be waged by individuals, and it is not permissible for an individual or group to declare war against a state; rather, it is exclusively the sultan's authority. There is no jihad except under the banner of a legitimate ruler.

There are contracts of security between us and the Western countries that ISIS wants to wage war on, which are exemplified in the exchange of ambassadors through diplomatic relations. Furthermore, there is cooperation in many aspects of society including economics, manufacturing, agriculture, and others in which Muslims require the experience of more advanced nations. Millions of Muslim immigrants live in Western countries with security, enjoying the same rights as the natives. They live comfortably with a degree of religious and political freedom they may not find in Islamic countries.

Since the middle of the twentieth century, millions of Muslims migrated to Europe and the Americas escaping religious oppression in pursuit of knowledge or seeking a better future for themselves and their families. They were welcomed in these countries and received assistance in every manner despite the difference in their religion, language, culture, and customs. The vast majority of these countries supported immigrant Muslims without discriminating between them and the native citizens, so how can a Muslim return the favor by killing, stealing, and deceiving his sponsors? A God-fearing Muslim could never justify this type of treachery. To the contrary, Muslims were known throughout history as an honorable people who upheld their covenants, even if it brought themselves harm; this display of magnanimous character was one of the key factors in the spread of Islam.

There is no justification for Muslims to commit acts of terrorism in the Western countries in which they reside, even if they are oppressed or have limited freedom to practice their religion, such as being banned from wearing the hijab. The only methods they are permitted to employ to change such policies are those which are both legal and peaceful, without any transgression, violence, or otherwise illegal acts as established by the laws of the land. If they find it impossible to practice their religion or change the policies of the government, they should simply migrate to a different land where they have full freedom of worship.

CHAPTER XI

Legal Rulings Regarding Non-Muslims in Muslim Countries

IN A SIMILAR fashion to what was mentioned in the previous chapter, any foreign residents, tourists, students, diplomats, journalists, and aid workers who enter Muslims lands with security do so under a covenant and contract. Deceiving or harming them is impermissible. Likewise, kidnapping foreigners is forbidden[92] and any ransom taken in exchange is unlawful.

Al-Bukhari narrates that the Prophet ﷺ said, "Whoever kills a non-Muslim under contract will never smell the scent of paradise."[93] He ﷺ also said, "When a Muslim offers protection to a non-Muslim, it is a covenant and it goes for all. Anyone who breaches this covenant shall have upon him a curse from Allah, the angels, and all mankind."[94]

Hafiz Abu al-Fadl al-'Asqalani said when commenting on the former narration, "Anyone who has a contract with the Muslims, whether by *jizya* (tax), by a truce from a sultan, or by security from a Muslim, is included."[95]

The presence of a leader is not a condition for offering security. If a non-Muslim enters Muslim lands by the security of one Muslim then all Muslims must fulfil that pledge, otherwise the claim of security would be treacherous and treachery is from the qualities of hypocrites.

Here one realizes the extent to which ISIS has violated the laws of Islam, where they combine killing and treachery by kidnapping and murdering foreign aid workers and reporters who have not committed any crime, and then gleefully broadcast their brutality to the masses.

Al-Nawawi said, "What is meant by *dhimma* (pact of protective custody for non-Muslims) here is security, meaning that the security of Muslims for non-Muslims is valid. If one of the Muslims gives him security, then it is unlawful for anyone else to expose him to harm as long as he is under the protection of a Muslim."[96] It is not permissible to kill a non-Muslim under contractual protection nor a non-Muslim combatant who is given security by a Muslim.

Amongst the rulings of non-Muslim citizens and those under contractual protection are that they are not to be exposed to any harm and it is impermissible to destroy any wine or swine a non-Muslim owns. Imam Kamal al-Din Ibn al-Humam went further and said, "Backbiting him is unlawful just as backbiting a Muslim is unlawful."[97] Ibn 'Abidin adopted this opinion in his sub-commentary known as *Radd al-Muhtar*, explaining that oppression against a non-Muslim citizen is worse, saying that it is "because with the contractual *dhimma* (pact) everything obligatory towards [one of] us is obligatory towards him, so if backbiting a Muslim is impermissible then backbiting him is [also] impermissible. In fact, they [scholars] said that oppression against a non-Muslim citizen is worse."[98] Ibn Hajar al-Haytami mentioned the same in his book entitled Deterrents from Committing Enormities.[99] The Prophetic statements prohibiting oppression against non-Muslim citizens are mass-transmitted and beyond doubt (*mutawatir*).[100]

Insulting a non-Muslim citizen is a sin requiring a punishment less than the prescribed penalties. It is related in the original text of Ibn 'Abidin's sub-commentary that 'Alā' al-Din al-Haskafi said, "If a Muslim swears at a non-Muslim citizen, he should be punished since he has committed a sin." By non-Muslim citizen (*dhimmi*), every non-Muslim is included whether in our lands or theirs.

The jurists went a step further by deeming it impermissible to even say to a Jew, Christian, or Zoroastrian, "O infidel (*kafir*)!" or "you are an infidel" if it hurts him. A Muslim should be punished for this as he has committed a sin.[101] This is only due to the fact that Islam aspires to a life of co-existence based upon respecting others in their faith, feelings, and rights. Islam was a pioneer in this before there were calls for dialogue between faiths to diffuse tension, or before the call to give religious minorities their rights.

In the book *al-Iqna'*, which is a reliable book for fatwa in the Hanbali legal school, it states, "Whoever curses a non-Muslim citizen should receive a light punishment." The commentator Imam Mansur al-Bahuti explains this, "It is because a non-Muslim citizen is under protection and [tainting] his honor is impermissible." He goes on further to say that cursing a specific individual is impermissible even if he is a non-Muslim citizen (*dhimmi*), stating that, "As for specifically cursing a person, its impermissibility is apparent even if he is a non-Muslim citizen who committed a crime."[102]

In the encyclopaedias of Islamic law, there are countless examples of Islam striving for justice and equality between all citizens, as well as with enemies at times of peace and truce.

Conclusion

Changing the Conditions which Help Extremism Grow

BEFORE I FINISH this fatwa, I would like to direct the attention of the international community who are fighting ISIS to four points that I see as the most important reasons which have fuelled the growth of extremism and assisted in recruiting more fighters in its ranks.

First, it is incumbent upon the government of Iraq to remove oppression from the Sunni population, to stop discriminating against them, and to give them their complete political rights, as extremists exploit the suffering of Sunnis to expand in that region.

Second, it is incumbent upon Bashar al-Assad's regime in Syria to cede authority to the people as his regime's barbaric crimes against its citizenry is still the most important factor feeding extremism and giving birth to terrorism in the region. The failure of the international community to assist the Syrian people to displace the regime has opened the door to an influx of foreign fighters into Syria, which has complicated the cause of the Syrian people and increased their suffering.

Third, the international community must respect the rights of Muslim minorities, especially in countries like Myanmar (Burma) and the Central African Republic, where images of Muslim persecution in those countries fuel the feelings of revenge amongst extremists, lend credence to the idea of a conspiracy against Islam, and validate the concern among Muslims that their blood is cheap.

Fourth, while we acknowledge the differences in values and cultures between the East and the West and call Muslims to respect Western societies and cultures, Western countries must also respect Muslim values and sacred figures and reconsider the boundaries of free speech.

This should be done in light of weighing benefits and harms, especially when its consequences affect the entire world.

Persisting in offending the Prophet of Islam, for example, will never make our war on terror an easy task, but rather it will exacerbate the feeling of anger among Muslims. This is where malicious terrorist organizations like ISIS emerge to exploit this anger, fan the flames of hatred and revenge, and earn sympathy from lay Muslims.

⌒

In light of this exposition, it is clear that the followers of ISIS do not represent Islam whatsoever. They have in fact left Islam, and the so-called state known as ISIS is certainly not Islamic and could not be further from the rulings of Islamic law. The actions of ISIS are simply a series of crimes perpetrated in the name of Islam. It has attempted in vain to find supporting evidences in the rich Islamic tradition to misguide people into thinking it is defending Islam and reviving the state of Islam. ISIS is led by a handful of criminals and ignorant extremists who are thirsty for blood and living with envy, hatred and rebelliousness.

Islam disavows ISIS. The Messenger of Allah ﷺ disavows ISIS. The scholars disavow ISIS.

The followers of ISIS do not want to adhere to Islamic law but rather they want to twist Islamic law to conform to their fantasies. To this end, they pick and choose the evidences that corroborate their misguidance, despite being weak or abrogated. They do not want to follow the Sunna of the Prophet ﷺ, but rather to twist the Sunna according to their desires.

In order to confirm this view of ISIS, I draw your attention to the statement of an ISIS figure, Kamal Zarruq, who said in a Friday sermon delivered in Tel Abyad, south of Syria, openly expressing disbelief and shamelessly insulting the Prophet ﷺ, "If Muhammad was with us he would have joined ISIS."[103] He had total belief in his statement, supplementing it by saying, "By Allah I'm not bothered about this statement. Indeed I am certain that we are upon truth." This statement warrants a judgement of clear disbelief in Islam and an insult to the Prophet of Islam ﷺ, after which no repentance is accepted. They deem themselves above the Prophet ﷺ and see the Prophet ﷺ, and all Prophets by extension, as their followers, declaring themselves as the lawgivers. Such statements are unmistakably proclamations of disbelief. It is therefore no surprise to see them twisting the Shariah and distorting Islam.

As with all oppressors, Allah Almighty has promised that their demise is imminent. As believers and concerned citizens of the world, we must do our part, working in conjunction with the international community to prevent the proliferation of ISIS, the ideology that begets such extremist groups, and the conditions that foster their growth.

Servant of the Sacred Knowledge
MUHAMMAD AL-YAQOUBI
Sha'ban 1435 AH

Notes

1. Already, al-Qaeda and other jihadist groups are rallying to the ISIS flag to face the "War of the Cross" waged against them. And already, western-backed rebels are becoming "traitors," and those who "deal with the West" (Abdullah of Saudi Arabia, UAE and Bahrain) are becoming "part of the West" -- i.e. apostates. Was this not somehow foreseeable? ISIS is using us to give it what it wants: wide Islamic mobilization, the de-legitimization of allied Arab leaders, and an inchoate "war" with no strategy or "end game" – a process Obama is in fact facilitating." See http://www.huffingtonpost.com/alastair-crooke/how-isis-is-using-us_b_5877570.html (last accessed August 24, 2015)

2. See UNHR: Iraq: UN report documents human rights violations of increasingly sectarian nature, http://www.ohchr.org/EN/NewsEvents/Pages/DisplayNews.aspx?NewsID=15598&LangID=E#sthash.c34Hpyje.dpuf (last accessed August 19, 2015).

3. http://www.businessinsider.com/revealed-the-oil-middleman-between-the-syrian-regime-and-isis-2015-3 (last accessed August 24, 2015); http://www.telegraph.co.uk/news/worldnews/middleeast/syria/10585391/Syrias-Assad-accused-of-boosting-al-Qaeda-with-secret-oil-deals.html (last accessed August 24, 2015)

4. Suicide bombers.

5. *DABIQ*, From Hypocrisy To Apostasy. Rabi' al-Akhir 1436.

6. *DABIQ*, The Return of Khilafah. Ramadan 1435.

7. DABIQ, The World Has Divided Into Two Camps. Ramadan 1435.

8. DABIQ, The Flood. Ramadan 1435.

, The Extinction of the Grayzone. Rabi' al-Akhir 1435.

IQ, They Plot And Allah Plots. Sha'ban 1436.

aghut refers to idols or things worshipped besides Allah. It is a term applied by ISIS and similar groups to governments that rule by manmade laws. [ed.]

12 That is, acts that create mass casualties. [ed.]

13 Sunni Muslims. [ed.]

14 Group or organization. [ed.]

15 DABIQ, From Hijra to Khilafah. Ramadan 1435.

16 DABIQ, The Concept of Imamah is From the Millah of Ibrahim. Ramadan 1435.

17 DABIQ, The Widespread Ignorance Amongst the People. Ramadan 1435.

18 Ibid.

19 DABIQ, Islam is The Religion of the Sword Not Pacifism. Rabi' al-Akhir 1436.

20 ISN Islamic State News, Smashing The Borders of Tawaghit. Sha'ban 1435.

21 DABIQ, Remaining & Expanding. 1436 Muharram,

22 Ibid.

23 The term *kuffar asliyyin* refers to people who have never embraced Islam, in contradistinction to apostates who were once Muslims but left the religion. [ed.]

24 DABIQ, Dismantling a Khariji Cell. Rabi' al-Awwal 1436.

25 DABIQ, The Extinction of the Grayzone. Rabi' al-Akhir 1436.

26 Ibid.

27 DABIQ, Shariah Alone Will Rule Africa, 1436 Jumada al-Akhira.

28 DABIQ, They Plot And Allah Plots. Sha'ban 1436.

29 DABIQ, And Allah is the Best of Plotters. Sha'ban 1436.

30 DABIQ, They Plot And Allah Plots. Sha'ban 1436.

31 Abu Dharr narrated that the Messenger of Allah ﷺ said, "Truly after me there is [an in another wording "there shall be"] from my nation a people who read the Quran though it does not pass their throats. They shall pass out of the religion just as an arrow passes out of the prey and shall never return to it. They are the worst of both men and animals." Recorded by Muslim in the section of

Zakat under the chapter entitled, "The Khawarij Are the Worst of Both Men and Animals" (vol. 3 p. 116).

32 Several companions narrated this description from the Prophet ﷺ, amongst them are 'Ali, Ibn 'Abbas, Ibn Mas'ud, Abu Sa'id al-Khudri, Anas b. Malik, Jabir b. 'Abdillah, Sahl b. Hunayf, 'Uqbah b. 'Amir al-Juhani, Abu Barzah al-Aslami, Abu Bakrah Nufay' b. al-Harith b. Kalada, and Abu Dharr. Some of them narrate, "They shall pass out of Islam." See their narrations in *al-Musnad* of Imam Ahmad b. Hanbal (vol. 1 pp. 88, 92, 131, 147, 151, 160, 256, 404; vol. 3 pp. 5, 15, 33, 52, 56, 60, 64, 65, 67,73, 159, 179, 224, 353-355, 476; vol. 4 pp. 145, 422, 425; vol. 5 pp. 42,176). The hadith of 'Ali is recorded by al-Bukhari, cf. (9). The hadith of Abu Sa'id al-Khudri is recorded by al-Bukhari in the section "Asking Apostates and Rebels to Repent and Fighting Them," in the chapter entitled "Killing the Khawarij and Heretics After Establishing Proof Against them" (vol. 9 pp. 16–17). Muslim records it in the section of *Zakat* under the chapter entitled, "Recounting the Khawarij and Their Qualities" (vol. 3 p. 112).

33 Abu Sa'id al-Khudri and Anas b. Malik narrated that the Messenger of Allah ﷺ said, "There shall be in my nation difference and disunion, a people who speak wondrously but act poorly, who recite the Quran though it does not pass their throats. They shall pass out of the religion just as an arrow passes out of the prey. They shall not return until it returns to its nocking point [i.e., they will never return]. They are the worst of both men and animals. Glad tidings to whoever kills them and whomsoever they kill. They call to the book of Allah though they do not belong to it in the slightest. Whoever fights them is closer to Allah than them." The Companions said, "O Messenger of Allah! What is their distinguishing feature?" He said, "Head shaving." Recorded by Abu Dawud in *al-Sunan* (see *Jami' al-Usul* by Ibn al-Athir, vol. 10 p. 79), and recorded by Imam Ahmed in *al-Musnad* (vol. 3 p. 224).

34 Abu Umama al-Bahili was narrated saying, "The worst of those who are killed under the sky, the best martyr is the one whom they kill, the dogs of hell, they were Muslims who became

disbelievers." The narrator said, "O Abu Umama! Is this what you are saying? He said, "Rather I heard it from the Messenger of Allah ﷺ." Recorded by al-Tirmidhi (§3003) in his *Jami'* under the chapter entitled, "Exegesis of *Surat Al 'Imran*" and Ibn Majah under the chapter entitled, "Recounting the Khawarij" (see *Jami' al-Usul* by Ibn al-Athir (vol. 2 p. 68), and recorded by Imam Ahmad in *al-Musnad* (vol. 5 pp. 253, 257). Al-Hakim recorded it in *al-Mustadrak* (vol. 2 pp. 149–150) and al-Dhahabi agreed with him. Abu Umama was with 'Ali ﷺ in Siffin and later settled in the Levant.

35 cf. (3).

36 Narrated in the hadith of Abu Umama, cf. (4). In the narration of al-Hakim in *al-Mustadrak* it is "the dogs of Hell."

37 Narrated by 'Abdullah b. 'Amr in which he said that 'Umar b. al-Khattab said, "O Messenger of Allah, shall we not kill him?" He said, "No, invite him as he shall have a following who seek the extremities of the religion until they leave it just as the arrow leaves the prey. Its arrowhead is inspected and nothing is found. Then the arrow shaft and nothing is found. Then its nock and nothing is found. It has left the dung and blood behind." Recorded by Imam Ahmad in *al-Musnad* (vol. 2 p. 219). This was documented by al-Haythami in *Majma' al-Zawa'id* (vol. 6 pp. 227–228) who said that Ahmad and al-Tabarani recorded it in brief and that Ahmad's narrators are trustworthy. It is narrated in the hadith of Abu Sa'id al-Khudri, "They seek the extremities of the religion" recorded in *al-Musnad* (vol. 3 p. 33), and in the hadith of Anas b. Malik recorded in *al-Musnad* (vol. 3 p. 159). It is a description of humiliation due to the reprehensibility that has been narrated regarding those who seek extremities in the religion. Al-Bukhari, in the section "Clinging to the Book and Sunna," has a chapter entitled, "What Is Disliked Regarding Seeking Extremities, Quarrelling in Knowledge, Extremism in Religion and Innovation." (vol. 9 p. 97)

38 'Ubaydullah b. Abi Rafi', the freed servant of the Messenger of Allah ﷺ, narrated that when the Haruriyya [another name for the Khawarij] revolted while he was with 'Ali b. Abi Talib, they

would say, "There is no rule except for Allah." 'Ali then said, "A word of truth though evil is intended by it. The Messenger of Allah ﷺ described a people and truly I see their traits in these. They speak the truth with their tongues though it does not pass this"—and he pointed to his throat. "They," he said, "are amongst the most hated of creation by Allah..." This was recorded by Muslim in the section of *Zakat,* under the chapter entitled, "Insistence on Killing the Khawarij" (vol. 3 p. 116). See *Jami' al-Usul* by Ibn al-Athir (vol. 10 pp. 79-80).

39 Recorded by al-Bukhari in the section "Virtues of the Quran," under the chapter entitled, "Whoever Acts Ostentatiously by Reciting the Quran, Devours It, or Boasts of It" (vol. 6 p. 197), and in in the section "Asking Apostates and Rebels to Repent and Fighting Them," in the chapter entitled "Killing the Khawarij and Heretics After Establishing Proof Against Them" (vol. 9 p. 16). Also recorded by Muslim in the section on *Zakat,* in the chapter entitled, "Recounting the *Khawarij* and Their Qualities" (vol. 3 p. 114), and Abu Dawud (§4767), al-Nasa'i (vol. 7 p. 119), and others.

40 'Abdullah b. 'Umar narrated, "I heard the Messenger of Allah ﷺ saying, "There shall emerge a people from my nation, acting poorly, reciting the Quran though it does not pass their throats." Yazid said, "I only know that he said, 'Any one of you shall belittle his actions alongside their actions. They shall kill the people of Islam, so when they emerge kill them, then when they emerge kill them, then when they emerge kill them. Glad tidings to whoever kills them and glad tidings to whomever they kill. Whenever a generation of theirs emerges Allah Almighty severs it.' The Messenger of Allah ﷺ repeated that twenty or more times while I listened." Recorded by Ibn Majah in the introduction to *al-Sunan*, under the chapter entitled, "Recounting the Khawarij " (vol. 1 p. 61 §174) and by Imam Ahmad in *al-Musnad* (vol. 2 p. 84). 'Abdullah b. 'Amr narrated, "I heard the Messenger of Allah ﷺ say, 'Indeed a people shall come into being amongst you who read the Quran though it does not pass their throats. Whenever a generation of theirs emerges it

is severed'—this he mentioned twenty or more times and then said, 'until the last of them shall emerge with the Anti-Christ.'" Recorded by Imam Ahmad in *al-Musnad* (vol. 2 pp. 199, 209).

41   http://www.cnn.com/2014/08/19/world/meast/isis-james-foley/ (last accessed August 12, 2015).

42   https://www.washingtonpost.com/world/syria-tribal-revolt-against-islamic-state-ignored-fueling-resentment/2014/10/20/25401beb-8de8-49f2-8e64-c1cfbee45232_story.html (last accessed August 12 , 2015)

43   http://www.theguardian.com/world/2014/nov/16/us-confirmation-isis-murder-peter-kassig (last accessed August 12 , 2015)

44   "In burning the crusader pilot alive and burying him under a pile of debris, the Islamic State carried out a just form of retaliation for his involvement in the crusader bombing campaign which continues to result in the killing of countless Muslims who, as a result of these airstrikes, are burned alive and buried under mountains of debris..." DABIQ (issue 7, p. 6)

45   "... many of those who say 'La ilaha illallah' have fallen into different shades of shirk at all levels, including shirk in tawassul and du'a, shirk in obedience, ruling and legislation, and shirk in love, support and allegiance." DABIQ (issue 2, p. 10)

46   http://www.nytimes.com/2014/10/26/world/middleeast/horror-before-the-beheadings-what-isis-hostages-endured-in-syria.html (last accessed August 12 , 2015)

47   http://www.washingtonpost.com/news/morning-mix/wp/2014/06/13/isis-beheadings-and-the-success-of-horrifying-violence/ (last accessed August 12 , 2015)

48   http://www.independent.co.uk/news/world/middle-east/isis-publishes-penal-code-listing-amputation-crucifixion-and-stoning-as-punishments--and-vows-to-vigilantly-enforce-it-9994878.html (last accessed August 12 , 2015)

49   https://www.hrw.org/news/2014/07/19/iraq-isis-abducting-killing-expelling-minorities (last accessed August 12 , 2015)

50   http://www.huffingtonpost.com/2014/07/25/isis-jonah-tomb_n_5620520.html

(last accessed August 12 , 2015)

51 http://www.iraqinews.com/features/urgent-isil-destroys-mosque-biblical-jonah-prophet-yunus/ (last accessed August 12 , 2015)

52 http://www.worldbulletin.net/news/156360/isil-destroys-historical-church-in-mosul (last accessed August 12 , 2015)

53 http://www.bbc.com/news/world-middle-east-33369701 (last accessed August 12 , 2015)

54 http://www.bbc.com/news/world-middle-east-33369701 (last accessed August 12 , 2015)

55 "The apostatizing hypocritical factions are those who moved from the grayzone to the camp of kufr by aiding the blatant murtaddin – the secularist and democratic factions – against the mujahidin. They followed this treachery by making political declarations of kufr themselves. As for the blatant murtaddin who had publicly called to democracy (the secularist and democratic factions), then they were never in the grayzone to begin with except in the eyes of the most extreme Murji'ah; but these democratic factions have become further exposed by the crusade they have rushed to support..." DABIQ (issue 7, p. 64 fn.)

56 "It was as if they weren't aware that amongst those who are liable to have their blood shed for the sake of this cause are fellow Muslims who testify that la ilaha illallah. However, these Muslims are renegades whom it's permissible to fight, and for no reason other than the fact that they refuse to give bay'ah (allegiance) to one imam or another." DABIQ (issue 1, p. 24)

57 "Accordingly, the Islamic State dealt with this group as the majority of fuqaha' have indicated how mushrikin should be dealt with. Unlike the Jews and Christians, there was no room for jizyah payment. Also, their women could be enslaved unlike female apostates who the majority of the fuqaha ¯' say cannot be enslaved1 and can only be given an ultimatum to repent or face the sword. After capture, the Yazidi women and children were then divided according to the Shari'ah amongst the fighters of the Islamic State who participated in the Sinjar operations, after one fifth of the slaves were transferred to the Islamic State's authority

to be divided as khums. This large-scale enslavement of mushrik families is probably the first since the abandonment of this Shari'ah law..." DABIQ (issue 4, p. 15)

58 http://www.hrw.org/news/2015/04/14/iraq-isis-escapees-describe-systematic-rape (last accessed August 12 , 2015)

59 http://www.amnesty.org.uk/sites/default/files/escape_from_hell_-_torture_and_sexual_slavery_in_islamic_state_captivity_in_iraq_-_english_2.pdf (last accessed August 12 , 2015)

60 http://edition.cnn.com/2014/06/25/world/meast/syria-isis-schoolboys/index.html (last accessed August 12 , 2015)

61 "[A] person who ignorantly practices any major shirk or totally abandons practice of the religion's other four pillars (prayer, zakah, siyam, and hajj) can never be considered Muslim." DABIQ (issue 7, p. 23 fn. 6)

62 "...many of those who say "La ilaha illallah" have fallen into different shades of shirk at all levels, including shirk in tawassul and du'a', shirk in obedience, ruling and legislation, and shirk in love, support and allegiance." DABIQ (issue 2, p. 10)

63 "In addition to that, he tried to force every apostate group present in Iraq into an all- out war with Ahlus-Sunnah. So he targeted the Iraqi apostate forces (army, police, and intelligence), the Rafidah (Shia markets, temples, and militias), and the Kurdish secularists (Barzani and Talabani partisans). In his speech titled "Hadha Bayanullin-Nasi wa li Yundharu Bih" (This Is a Declaration for the People That They May Be Warned by It), he threatened war on any Sunni tribe, party, or assembly that would support the crusaders. Then when some so-called 'Islamists' entered into the democratic political process – ignoring what it entails of clear- cut major shirk – he officially declared war on them in his speech titled 'Wa li Tastabina Sabilul-Mujrimin' (And Thus the Way of the Criminals Becomes Evident)." DABIQ (issue 1, p. 37)

64 "The Islamic State – on account of what Allah has blessed it with of victory, consolidation and establishing the religion – is regarded as an unquestionable imamah. As such, anyone who rebels against its authority inside its territory is considered a

renegade, and it is permissible to fight him after establishing the hujjah against him (i.e. clarifying his error to him with proof).'" DABIQ (issue 1, p. 27)

65 https://www.washingtonpost.com/world/middle_east/al-qaeda-disavows-any-ties-with-radical-islamist-isis-group-in-syria-iraq/2014/02/03/2c9afc3a-8cef-11e3-98ab-fe5228217bd1_story.html (last accessed August 16, 2015). See also http://www.cnn.com/2014/11/21/world/meast/al-qaeda-yemen-isis/ (last accessed August 16, 2015).

66 "It was as if they weren't aware that amongst those who are liable to have their blood shed for the sake of this cause are fellow Muslims who testify that la ilaha illallah. However, these Muslims are renegades whom it's permissible to fight, and for no reason other than the fact that they refuse to give bay'ah (allegiance) to one imam or another." DABIQ (issue 1, p. 24)

67 Abu Bakr Muhammad b. al-Hasan al-Ajurri, *Kitab al-Shari'ah*, edited by 'Abdullah al-Damiji, 2nd edition (Riyadh: Dar al-Watn, 1420 AH) (vol. 1 p. 325).

68 Qadi Abu Bakr ibn al-'Arabi al-Maliki, *'Arida al-Ahwadhi Sharh Sahih al-Tirmidhi* (vol. 9 p. 38).

69 Al-Qurtubi, *al-Mufhim lima Ashkala min Talkhis Kitab Muslim* (vol. 3 p. 110).

70 Shaykh 'Abd al-'Aziz Ibn Baz, *Man Hum al-Khawarij*, http://www.binbaz.org.sa/mat/20688, (last accessed May 4, 2015).

71 *Open Letter to al-Baghdadi*, http://www.lettertobaghdadi.com/ar/, (last accessed May 4, 2015).

72 The hadith of Ibn 'Abbas debating the Khawarij, recorded by al-Hakim in *al-Mustadrak* (vol. 2 pp. 189-190 §2656), agreed by al-Dhahabi regarding its authenticity, in which there is, "so two thousand of them returned." We mentioned what Imam Ahmad recorded in *al-Musnad* from the narration of 'Abdullah b. Shaddad (vol. 1 p. 87).

73 *Sahih al-Bukhari* (vol. 9 p. 16).

74 Ibn Battal, *Sharh Sahih al-Bukhari* (vol. 8 p. 590).

75 A portion of a long hadith recorded by Imam Ahmad in his *Musnad* (vol. 1 p. 87) and Abu Ya'la al-Musili in his *Musnad* (vol. 1

p. 369 §474).

76 Abu 'Ubayd al-Qasim Ibn Sallam, *Kitab al-Amwal* (pp. 254–255).

77 Recorded by al-Bukhari in the *Sahih* from the hadith of Ibn 'Abbas, in the section on the Prophets, in the chapter of "The Words of Allah Almighty ❰*And as for 'Ad, they were destroyed by a furious Wind, exceedingly violent*❱ (vol. 4 p. 137); and in the section of Expeditions, in the chapter entitled, "Sending 'Ali b. Abi Talib and Khalid b. al-Walid to Yemen before the farewell pilgrimage" (vol. 5 p. 162) with the words "as Thamud was killed"; and in the section on Divine Oneness, in the chapter entitled, "The Words of Allah Almighty ❰*The angels and the spirit ascend unto him*❱" (vol. 9 p. 127); and documented by Muslim in the *Sahih*, in the section of *Zakat*, in the chapter entitled, "Recounting the Khawarij " (vol. 3 p. 110).

78 cf. (9).

79 Imam Ahmad, *al-Musnad* (Beirut: Mu'assasa al-Risala) (§5562).

80 Ibn Taymiyya, *al-Fatawa al-Kubra* (vol. 3 p. 536).

81 Ibn Hubayra, *al-Ifsah 'an Ma'ani al-Sihah* (vol. 1 p. 280).

82 Narrated in the hadith of Abu Umama, "The best martyr is the one whom they kill," cf. (4), also recorded by Al-Hakim in *Al-Mustadrak* (vol. 2 p. 188 §2654).

83 Recorded by al-Bukhari in the *Sahih*, in the section on Corporal Punishments, under the chapter entitled "Stoning the Woman Made Pregnant by Fornication If She Was Chaste" (vol. 8 p. 169). Ibn al-Athir, in *al-Nihaya fi Gharib al-Hadith wa al-Athar*, said, "The word *al-taghirrah* (deadly risk) is a verbal noun meaning to throw someone into danger. It is from the word *al-taghrir* (deadly risk) just like *al-ta'illah* is from *al-ta'lil*. The meaning of the hadith is that the proper manner regarding the oath of allegiance is for it to originate out of consultation and agreement; so if two men proceed independently without a group, and one gives the oath of allegiance to the other, then that is openly splitting the public and rejecting the majority." (vol. 3 p. 156). The accuracy of "*taghirrat^an*" is from *Sahih al-Bukhari*, the Yuniniyyah edition.

84 http://www.longwarjournal.org/archives/2014/05/jailed_jihadist_ideo.php (last accessed August 16 , 2015)

85 Recorded by Muslim in the section of "Fighting and Marching," under the chapter entitled "The Dislike of Seeking Assistance from a Non-Muslim in a Military Expedition" (vol. 5 p. 201), in which the hadith ends with, "He said, 'Then he returned and met him in the desert so he said what he said the first time, "Do you believe in Allah and His Messenger?" He said, "Yes." The Messenger of Allah 🕮 said to him, "Then go."'"

86 Al-Nawawi, *al-Minhaj Sharh Sahih Muslim Ibn al-Hajjaj* (vol. 12 p. 199).

87 See for example the fatwa of Shaykh 'Abd al-'Aziz Ibn Baz regarding the permissibility of seeking assistance from a non-Muslim out of necessity, http://www.binbaz.org.sa/mat/254, (last accessed May 4, 2015).

88 http://www.cnn.com/2015/06/26/africa/tunisia-terror-attack/ (last accessed August 16, 2015)

89 Recorded by al-Bukhari in the *Sahih*, narrated by Ibn 'Umar in the section of "Manners," under the chapter entitled, "What People Are Called by Their Fathers" (vol. 8 p. 41), and in other numerous places. Also recorded by Muslim in the *Sahih* in the section of "Fighting and Marching," under the chapter entitled, "The Impermissibility of Treachery" (vol. 5 pp. 141–142).

90 Shaykh 'Abd al-'Aziz Ibn Baz, *Majmu' al-Fatawa* (vol. 7 p. 364; vol. 18 p. 436; vol. 25 p. 373).

91 Ibn 'Abidin, *Radd Al-Muhtar 'ala al-Durr al-Mukhtar* (vol. 4 p. 166).

92 See the fatwa I published in 2012 regarding the impermissibility of kidnapping foreigners, amongst other fatwas, http://www.joshualandis.com/blog/wp-content/uploads/Yaqoubi-fatwas-for-the-uprising.pdf, (last accessed May 4, 2015).

93 Recorded by al-Bukhari in the section of "Fighting," under the chapter entitled, "The Sin of the One Who Kills a Non-Muslim Under Contract for No Crime" (vol. 4 p. 99); and in the chapter entitled, "Blood Money"; and in the chapter entitled, "The Sin of the One Who Kills a Non-Muslim Citizen for No Crime" (vol. 9 p. 12), which concludes with, "and indeed its fragrance is found spanning a distance traversed over forty years."

94 Recorded by al-Bukhari, narrated by 'Ali in the section of "Tax
(*jizya*)," in the chapters entitled, "Tax (*jizya*) and Truce (*muwa-da'a*)"; "The Pact (*dhimma*) and Neighbourhood of Muslims Is
One, the Lowest of Them Fulfils It" (vol. 4 p. 100); "The Sin
of the One Who Enters into a State Contract then Commits
Treason" (vol. 4 p. 102); and in other places, in which it is said,
"When a Muslim offers protection to a non-Muslim it is a covenant and it goes for all. Anyone who breaches this covenant shall
have upon him a curse from Allah, the angels, and all mankind.
No payment or compensation shall be accepted from him."

95 Hafiz Abu al-Fadl Ibn Hajar al-'Asqalani, *Fath al-Bari Sharh Sahih
al-Bukhari* (vol. 12 p. 259).

96 Al-Nawawi, *al-Minhaj Sharh Sahih Muslim Ibn al-Hajjaj* (vol. 9 p.
144).

97 Kamal al-Din Ibn al-Humam, *Fath al-Qadir Sharh al-Hidaya* (vol.
6 p. 24).

98 Ibn 'Abidin, *Radd Al-Muhtar 'ala al-Durr al-Mukhtar* (vol. 4 p.
171).

99 Ibn Hajar al-Haytami, *al-Zawajir 'an Iqtiraf al-Kaba'ir* (vol. 2 p.
27).

100 Sayyid Muhammad b. Ja'far al-Kittani, *Nazm al-Mutanathir min
al-Hadith al-Mutawatir* (Fez: al-Matba'a al-Mawlawiyya, 1328 AH)
(p. 107), in which he said regarding the narrations prohibiting
the oppression of non-Muslim citizens, that "Al-Mawwaq mentioned them being of an unquestionable veracity (*tawatur*) in the
commentary of *Mukhtasar Khalil*... relating from Sahnun."

101 Ibn 'Abidin, *al-Durr al-Mukhtar Ma'a Aslihi Tanwir al-Absar* (vol.
3 p. 188). See these words, as well as the words of al-Haskafi
which precede it, and Ibn 'Abidin's agreement to it.

102 Shaykh Mansur b. Yunus al-Bahuti al-Hanbali, *Kashshaf al-Qana'
'an Matn al-Iqna'* (vol. 6 pp. 125-126), in the chapter of "Honor-
ing."

103 See these words in a Friday sermon delivered by the Tunisian
Kamal Zarruq in the following clip, minute 14: https://www.
youtube.com/watch?v=2hOks_nUmzY, (last accessed May 4,
2015).

Appendix

On Minorities in Syria
Interview with Shaykh Muhammad al-Yaqoubi
by Matthew Barber, May 31, 2015*

SHEIKH MUHAMMAD AL-YAQOUBI is a respected Sufi scholar and teacher from Damascus who has been an outspoken voice against IS and other extremist groups in Syria. Throughout the course of the uprising, he has been consulted by rebel fighters seeking guidance regarding their conduct in the war. In this capacity, the Sheikh has provided numerous fatwas against acts of extremism, violence against civilians, sectarian violence, and the killing of prisoners. Sheikh Yaqoubi has previously been interviewed for Syria Comment, and more information on his background and activities can be found in that article.

This past week, Sheikh Yaqoubi published a short book containing a detailed religious argument against the behavior and tactics of IS. The first of its kind, the book is entitled *The Obligation to Fight ISIS: A Detailed Fatwa Proving That ISIS Have Strayed from Islam, Opposed Shari'ah and That Fighting Them is Obligatory*. (The title of the Arabic version is: إنقاذُ الأُمَّة: فتو مفصلة في إثبات أن داعش خوارج وأن قتالهم واجب) A strong refutation of IS' ideology, this work is designed to influence Syrian fighters against IS as well as to curb IS' recruitment of Muslim youth around the world. It can also serve to encourage IS fighters to leave the organization. An Arabic version of the book has just been

* Original interview found at http://www.joshualandis.com/blog/sheikh-muhammad-al-yaqoubi-responds-to-al-julanis-al-jazeera-interview/ (last accessed August 20, 2015)

published in Turkey and is available here†; an English version is forthcoming. The book refutes IS on theological grounds for many aspects of its practice and positions, including their revival of slavery practices [...]

Also this past week, al-Jazeera ran an in-depth interview with Abu Mohammed al-Julani, the leader of Jabhat al-Nusra, Syria's al-Qaida organization. [...] Eyebrows have been raised by what has appeared as an attempt to improve Nusra's image as a more moderate alternative to IS that does not practice *takfir* (the practice of declaring a Muslim an unbeliever or apostate).

I spoke with Sheikh Yaqoubi on Friday. He shared with me his current efforts to ideologically combat IS, as well as his thoughts on the way that al-Jazeera handled the interview with al-Julani, the ranking representative of al-Qaida in Syria. Below is our discussion.

Sheikh Muhammad, what did you make of al-Jazeera's interview with Abu Mohammed al-Julani?

The interview was fifty minutes of mockery—a scandal for professional journalism. It is unbelievable that al-Jazeera is doing the dirty job of beautifying this man before tens of millions of viewers, ordinary Muslims, telling them that he is a good man who is doing a good job, helping the Syrian people, a good Muslim, a moderate Muslim—he's not! It was clear from the interview that the ideology of al-Nusra Front has not changed. Al-Julani twice confirmed his allegiance to al-Qaida, saying that he receives orders from its leader Dr. Aymenn [al-Zawahiri], and the interviewer never interjected any question about this. All the interviewer did was attempt to portray him as a nice man. He never asked him a critical question; he never challenged him.

What do you think is happening today that allows an important representative of al-Qaida to be featured on television in an accepting way by a mainstream voice of the media?

This question should be directed to Qatar's government. Why are they doing this?

† http://www.joshualandis.com/blog/wp-content/uploads/%D8%A5%D9%86%D9%82%D8%A7%D8%B0-%D8%A7%D9%84%D8%A3%D9%85%D8%A9.pdf (last accessed August 20, 2015)

The man clearly stated that he hasn't abandoned any of his principles. He only stated one thing that differs from his earlier positions: he says that he has received orders from al-Qaida leader Dr. Ayman to not target the West. This is the only real [ideological] change from what he conveyed in his earlier interview in 2013. Now they are just trying to get statements from him to the effect that "we do not do *takfir*." And yet in the same interview, he confirmed the extreme position that visiting shrines of saints is *kufr* or *shirk*, accusing people who visit shrines of being *mushrikiin* [those who "commit polytheism" by ascribing "partners" to God]. This means he is going to have to consider most Sunni Muslims apostates (which for him could mean having to kill them) because they have shrines of saints and visit them, such as our shrine for Ibn 'Arabi in the heart of Damascus, or in Konya the shrine for Mawlana Rumi, the most famous Muslim saint in the world. You have saints everywhere, from Morocco to South Africa, from Indonesia to Istanbul. All these Muslims are *mushrikiin*—non-Muslims, unbelievers—according to him? How can this be? This ideology is alien to the Syrian people and to the nature of Islam in Syria.

And ironically—or perhaps even sarcastically—they are trying to present him as so friendly toward [minority] sects.

As he said that Nusra will not kill Alawites or Druze.

Druze and Alawites—"if they don't fight us, if they don't work with Assad," then they will not kill them.

But he made changing their religion a prerequisite for this.

This is the key moment where the interviewer failed to interrupt to pose any hard questions. He [al-Julani] gave two conditions. The first was that they abandon Assad, or defect—and this is the understandable politics of war. But the second condition, at which the interviewer did not pause to question him, was, when talking about the Druze villages in Idlib, he said "we have sent them *du ' āt*" [proselytizers], people to correct their dogma or their Islam." And about Alawites, also he repeated that "if they accept Islam, we'll be fine with them." His approach to Druze and Alawites is that they should become Muslims and "then we will accept them," which differs from the long-established position adopted by Sunnis, such as the Hanafis and

Malikis, who accepted these groups and made them equal to the People of the Book. Al-Julani's position means that Alawites have the only the choices of converting to Islam or being killed; they would not even be extended the option of deportation.

Now, these Alawites and Druze, along with the Isma'ilis, have lived side by side with Sunni Muslims for over a thousand years, and Muslims did not attempt to erase, eradicate, or convert them, even though Muslims had power, as the rulers of the land, such as the Ottomans. This is because it is part of our legal system that these people could be treated as the People of the Book, which means they are full citizens of the countries where they live. It is in the Hanafi school, the Malaki school, it is even one opinion of Ahmad ibn Hanbal.

Now I understand the position of the Shafi'is, but it was never practiced, so why pick it up after all these centuries? While the majority of Muslim scholars say that even *mushrikiin* can be treated as the People of the Book? Imam Malik says this very clearly and so does Abu Hanifa. This was practiced for many centuries in Syria, so why now? Why turn the tables after all of this history and begin forcing people into Islam? Al-Julani wants to claim to be more loyal to Islam than the Muslims? More than the Ottomans, more than the Ayubids, more than the Abbasids, more than the Umayyads, more than the companions of the Prophet? This is very strange.

What Shafi'i position were you referring to?

The Shafi'is said that *jizya* can only be taken from Christians, Jews, and Magians [Zoroastrians], not from others. But this has never been practiced; the Shafi'i opinion on this has never been followed. We have a rule in *fiqh*: "Practice takes priority." In other words, the position of a *madhab* that becomes majority practice is validated, whereas an opposing position of another *madhab*, if not followed in a certain land, cannot be practiced there. Therefore the Shafi'i position on this has become invalid in Syria and neighboring countries because it was never adopted by any Muslim government. This is even echoed now by one of the major leaders of the current Salafi-jihadi movement, Abu Basir al-Tartusi, who states that the majority opinion on this is superior and should be practiced, and that all should be considered as People of the Book and should not be forced into Islam. He says this on his website.

Help me understand the difference between the Shafi'is on the one side, and the Hanafis and Malikis on the other. Both would agree that the option to pay *jizya* [rather than convert] is provided to the People of the Book, but the difference is about who is considered People of the Book?

The difference is about who can be *annexed* to the category, i.e. who can be merged into the People of the Book. It is about whether the "People of the Book" can be extended to include others who can be treated as the People of the Book, or not. Because in the past, when Muslims waged wars, they always offered the enemy three options before fighting: 1) the enemy could become Muslim, 2) they could remain non-Muslim and pay *jizya*, or 3) they could choose to fight. So for *mushrikiin*, the payment of *jizya* was not considered an option, in *some* opinions. But this was in regards to pagans among the Arabs. And the Hanafis, for example, and the Malikis on a larger scale, and even Ahmad ibn Hanbal according to one narration from him, all quote hadith from the Prophet, *salla Allah 'alayhi wa sallam*, reporting that when he sent people to fight pagan *mushrikiin*, he asked them to offer [to the latter] *all three* options. This means that even pagans cannot be forced into Islam, if they choose to pay *jizya*. There is also another hadith, one about the Magians, in Sahih Bukhari, that says "treat them like the People of the Book."

So from these proofs, these portions of hadith tradition, among others, scholars and Muslim jurists went on to say that all non-Muslim sects are annexed to the People of the Book. Let me state it clearly: Muslims were not keen on killing people. Muslims tried to save the lives of people under any pretext when any proof was available. They valued human life as God's creation, so when they found these clear proofs from among the words of the Prophet, they knew that Islam was a religion of mercy, because this is the higher purpose of the shari'a: mercy—not killing people, not harshness, not savagery.

This was the practiced pattern when Muslims had power. Today Muslims are weak, and a group like al-Nusra thinks that it can survive and become a superpower? This is ridiculous. Muslims were superpowers and controlled two thirds of the world, and they did not eradicate sects. They did not force them into Islam.

So when al-Julani mentioned placing *du ʿāt* among the Druze in Idlib, the interviewer did not interrupt him to question the practice.

He didn't challenge him at all. The way that al-Julani put it was "we sent missionaries, *du ʿāt*, to them, to correct for them their misunderstandings of Islamic dogma." But Julani is very aware that Druze are considered non-Muslims in books of theology. When they have freedom, they will identify as Druze.

There is no basis for forcing or pressuring others to enter Islam. In my new book on fighting ISIS, I mention that it is even forbidden to slander a Christian or another non-Muslim. Ibn Nujaim, one of the greatest scholars of *fiqh* and *uṣūl al-fiqh* in the Hanafi school, said that it is *haram*, forbidden, to say to a non-Muslim: "you *kāfir*,"because it upsets him, and you are not supposed to upset him by pointing out his difference in beliefs. This has been established in Islam for centuries. This is why when I once spoke in America at the Catholic University in Washington, I said that the concept of "tolerance" is alien to us, because tolerance means "bearing up with difficulty," i.e. doing a favor to the other. It is derived from the Latin verb *tolerare* which means "to endure pain." The Muslim relationship toward other sects was not based in "doing the favor" of tolerating them; they considered their separate beliefs as their right. Ibn ʿĀbidīn even says in his book *Radd Al-Muhtār* that oppression against non-Muslims is *worse* than oppression against Muslims.

So where do these people like Julani and Baghdadi come from? But this is what results when they destroy the twelve-century-long corpus of law of the four schools. This is what you get: everyone is implementing his own opinion. Everyone who carries a gun is now a *mujtahid* or a mufti, producing his own fatwas and acting as judge. They claim to act in reference to the book of Allah and the sunna of his Prophet, *salla Allah ʿalayhi wa sallam*, but they act according to their own understanding—or misunderstanding.

Islamic law develops [over time]. One of its beautiful characteristics is its flexibility. We have certain things that are constant over time, things like the pillars of Islam (prayer, fasting, and so forth), but then we have things that may evolve and change over time. There are a lot of these things, including *jizya*. It is not something that is rigidly defined, even though it is mentioned in the Qur'an.

So what do you think was the goal of that interview?

The purpose of the interview seemed to be just to elicit certain statements from al-Julani, particularly that "we don't do *takfir* to anyone," in a way that would increase his appeal to the public. It was a very dangerous interview.

And in the interview we don't really see a renouncing of *takfiri* practice or ideology?

No. And even if we did, there is more at issue with al-Qaida than the practice of *takfir*. For example, anyone who believes in democracy, for them, is a heretic. Another example: any Muslim ruler or country that enters an alliance with or seeks assistance from a non-Muslim country—they become unbelievers. There are many problems with al-Qaida, and the ideology is basically the same as that of ISIS, though ISIS has more extreme practices that have now made al-Qaida look nice. But we know that several thousand fighters moved from al-Nusra to ISIS.

Throughout the Syria conflict, every time a more radical group would appear, it would make the groups preceding it look less bad. People were concerned about Islamist groups, but after Nusra emerged, it began to appear as the bigger threat, making the other Islamists appear more moderate. After ISIS emerged, even Nusra began to look better, simply because it was not as extreme. People would perceive any opposition to whatever was the more extreme party as a good thing.

[laughing] Well if you believe in relativity, then that is the case! But we don't believe in relativity in this criminal arena. You can't say that a murderer who kills one person is a saint because someone else is killing more.

Let me ask you how you perceive the recent successes of Nusra and other Islamists. You are someone who wants to see a future peace in Syria, and you see both the Assad regime and Nusra as obstacles to that peace. So when you see Assad losing ground and Nusra or other Islamist groups gaining ground, do you interpret this as a positive or negative development, or neither?

Kicking the regime out of areas like Idlib is definitely good, but the ultimate solution for the crisis in Syria will be political. Sometimes people are happy that a piece of land is liberated, but then you see barrel bombs falling on people morning and night in that area, killing civilians and innocents. So it is good that the regime is now weaker, that more people are safe from the torture of the regime's prisons, from its special art in killing people. But what we need is to finally reach a political solution, where no fighting takes place.

Until now the regime has refused to talk seriously about any political solution. Do you think that with all its recent losses it may experience enough pressure that going to the negotiating table will become a real possibility?

I think that there may now be an agreement to get rid of Assad. Even Russia and Iran now believe that he has become a burden. But what system would follow? Of course Iran wants to guarantee its own interests in the country, and Russia wants to guarantee its interests. We do not want the major destruction of Damascus. So what is happening now is more military pressure on the regime to bring it to the negotiating table, where hopefully Assad could step down, an interim council would be created to which power would be handed over, and we would eventually witness a new Syria.

If that doesn't happen and the present fight continues to move, say to Latakia or Damascus, the destruction will just go on.

Let me say this: continuing the fight is no longer in the interest of Syrians.

Including the opposition.

Including the opposition because the opposition is not in power and is not represented by the people fighting on the ground. Those fighting are mainly extreme groups like ISIS and others who want to impose their own version of Islam, which is alien to the moderate Sunni Islam that the region has known for centuries. When you look at the four schools you realize that Islam is not about killing. For example, Islamic penalties could not be implemented in times of war, times of famine, times of ignorance and so forth. By putting Islamic penalties on hold, I am not challenging the book of Allah or the sunna. I am not challenging the books of *fiqh*. I am precisely following the reliable opinion of every school of law. Shari ʿ a is not about Islamic penalties; these extreme groups have reduced shari ʿ a to Islamic penalties, they have reduced shari ʿ a to *jizya* for non-Muslims. What about truthfulness, what about mercy, what about respect for citizens, what about protecting life? Islam is about these things.

Tell me about the new book you have written. It is a long fatwa about IS. What do you hope to accomplish with it?

First of all, I have seen a lot of need, from inside Syria and from around the world. From inside Syria I receive questions from fighters and commanders, from certain military groups, asking whether they should engage in the war against ISIS, asking whether ISIS are Muslims and whether they can fight against Muslims. And from non-Muslims around the world, you are aware how much fuss there is about ISIS and its crimes, especially after the burning alive of the Jordanian pilot Muaz al-Kasasbeh, Allah have mercy on him. So I saw the strong need [for an authoritative religious response to this], and there was only the one letter that was issued before, that I cosigned [www.lettertobaghdadi.com], but which did not go into enough detail regarding the proofs for the refutation of ISIS, but which mainly presented the basics. So I wrote this book directing the reader to the major positions held by ISIS, such as allegiance to Baghdadi and its validity, kidnapping, burning, slavery. Slavery is one of the major issues and I mentioned that as jurists, doctors of the law, from an Islamic point of view we are bound by international law on the issue, which we [Muslim countries] have signed, and Muslims must not breach their promises. Slavery should not be practiced and cannot be practiced; it is now forbidden in Islam for it to be practiced. This does not contradict the book of Allah or the sunna of the Prophet; it is rather in conjunction with them, because in Islam we are ordered to respect our covenants and contracts. Before the coming of Islam, the Prophet Mohammed participated in a covenant called the *Hilf al-Fudūl* that was made among tribes in Mecca to protect the oppressed. And after the message of Islam had come, the Prophet said that if he was again invited to such an accord that he would agree to it. So slavery in Islam is not obligatory; it is not the only option. Slavery was *one* option in Islam only because it was practiced in the world into which Islam came, and if the world comes to agree on abolishing it, we are bound by this. Even more so because our enemies do not enslave us. The only case in which slavery could still be applied would be if the world were to abolish the Declaration of Human Rights and begin to enslave Muslims. In such a scenario, Muslims could enslave their enemies as a kind of reciprocity. But this is impossible, an entirely imaginary hypothesis. There is now no place for slavery at all; it is out of the question.

Now when we spoke in 2013, you mentioned that many fighters were seeking your religious guidance, sometimes about relations with other groups, sometimes about fighting the regime. As the first sheikh to issue a fatwa validating resistance against the regime after its use of violence against the peaceful protesters, you played an important role in legitimizing the armed struggle of the opposition. I wonder now, in early 2015, whether similar numbers of fighters still consult you.

No. The reason is that many moderate fighters, for financial reasons or for lack of weapons and arms support, moved to join with al-Nusra or others. Three years ago there were so many military groups on the ground. Many of them were moderate and were fighting for a new Syria, and their goal was to take out the regime, not to create that form of a state which Nusra or ISIS is seeking to establish now. We all know that many Syrian fighters are now with ISIS or Nusra—they are well paid. Many looked at the international community with frustration, because they didn't see any support.

But some still contact me and I have received requests from some of the major military groups that still exist, from around the country. Their questions now are not about the regime but mainly concern fighting ISIS.

How much practical influence do you think that your book can have?

It is designed to impact three target groups. The first group is the fighters inside Syria.

And can it physically reach them?

Yes. One major rebel group inside Syria has already requested 10,000 copies of it. A second group has requested 5,000 copies. These are good signs. They want to educate their fighters, to discuss what is right and wrong, who represents Islam, and what kind of Islam is to be practiced. So this is very encouraging. And this is just in the first few days. By the way, I have published 25,000 copies [in Turkey, to be distributed to Syrian fighters] at my own expense. I have had no sponsors. But we are expecting that 100,000 copies will eventually be needed.

The second target group for the book is the youth outside of Syria, around the world, who are at risk for recruitment. They can be reached online, and when they read this book they will realize that ISIS does not represent Islam. Through this effort we will try to minimize the levels of recruitment. That is why there are versions in both Arabic and English.

And the third target group is academia and the media. I receive a lot of questions from both academia and the media about the legal stance of Islam and the various schools on these issues, and this work can help answer those questions from concerned observers.

We are hopeful about the potential of this book and feel that its reception is promising.

Bibliography

Abu Dawud al-Sijistani. *Sunan Abi Dawud*, n.p.

Ajurri, Abu Bakr al-. *Kitab Al-Shari'a*, n.p.

'Arabi, Qadi Abu Bakr ibn al-. *'Arida al-Ahwadhi Sharh Sahih Al-Tirmidhi*. Egypt, 1934.

'Asqalani, Hafiz Abu al-Fadl al-. *Fath al-Bari Sharh Sahih Al-Bukhari*. Beirut: Dar al-Ma'rifa, 1379 AH.

———. *Taghliq Al-Ta'liq*. Edited by Sa'id 'Abd al-Rahman Musa al-Qarafi. 2nd ed. Beirut: al-Maktab al-Islami, 1420 AH.

Bahuti, Mansur b. Yunus al-. *Kashshaf al-Qana' 'an Matn Al-Iqna'*. Edited by Hilal Musaylihi Mustafa Hilal. Riyadh: Matba'a al-Nasr al-Hadith, n.d.

Bukhari, Muhammad b. Isma'il al-. *al-Jami' al-Sahih*. 9 vols. Egypt: Matba'a al-Amiriyya al-Kubra, 1315 AH.

Hakim, Abu 'Abdillah al-. *Al-Mustadrak 'ala al-Sahihayn*. Beirut: Dar ibn Hazm, 2008.

Haytami, Ibn Hajar al-. *Al-Zawajir 'an Iqtiraf al-Kaba'ir*. 1st ed. Dar al-Fikr, 1407 AH.

Ibn al-Humam, Kamal al-Din Muhammad al-Siwasi. *Fath Al-Qadir Sharh al-Hidaya*. Dar al-Fikr, n.d.

Ibn 'Abd al-Barr. *Al-Istidhkar al-Jami' li Madhahib Fuqaha' al-Amsar*. Edited by 'Abd al-Mu'ti Amin Qal'aji. 30 vols. Cairo, 1414 AH.

Ibn 'Abidin. *Al-Durr al-Mukhtar Ma'a Aslihi Tanwir al-Absar*. Bulaq, Egypt, n.d.

———. *Radd al-Muhtar 'ala al-Durr al-Mukhtar*. 2nd ed. Beirut: Dar al-Fikr, 1412 AH.

Ibn Baz, Shaykh 'Abd al-'Aziz b. 'Abdillah. *Majmu' Al-Fatawa*, n.d.

Ibn Hammad, Nu'aym. *Kitab Al-Fitan*, n.d.

Ibn Hanbal, Imam Ahmad. *Al-Musnad*, n.d.

Ibn Hubayra. *Al-Ifsah 'an Ma'ani al-Sihah*. Edited by Fu'ad 'Abd al-Mun'im Ahmad. Dar al-Watn, 1417 AH.

Ibn Battal, Abu al-Hasan 'Ali. *Sharh Sahih al-Bukhari*. Edited by Yasir b. Ibrahim. 3rd ed. Riyadh: Maktaba al-Rushd, 1425 AH.

Ibn Majah, Abu 'Abdillah Muhammad ibn Yazid. *Sunan Ibn Majah*. Edited by Muhammad Fu'ad 'Abd al-Baqi. 2 vols. Egypt: Dar Ihya' al-Kutub al-'Arabiyya, 1372 AH.

Ibn Taymiyya. *Al-Fatawa al-Kubra*, n.p.

Jazari, Majd al-Din Ibn al-Athir al-. *Al-Nihaya fi Gharib al-Hadith wa al-Athar*. Egypt: al-Matba'a al-Khayriyya, 1322 AH.

————. *Jami' al-Usul fi Ahadith al-Rasul*. Edited by Shaykh 'Abd al-Qadir al-Arna'ut. 11 vols. Damascus: Matba'a Mallah, 1392 AH.

Naysaburi, Muslim b. Hajjaj al-. *Sahih al-Imam Muslim*. 8 vols. Istanbul: Dar Taba'a al-'Amira, 1320 AH.

Nasa'i, Ahmad b. Shu'ayb al-. *Sunan al-Nasa'i al-Sughra*. Al-Mujtaba, n.d.

Nawawi, Imam Yahya ibn Sharaf al-. *Al-Minhaj Sharh Sahih Muslim Ibn al-Hajjaj*. Cairo: al-Matba'a al-Misriyya, 1st ed., 1349 AH.

Qurtubi, Hafiz Abu al-'Abbas Ahmad b. 'Umar al-. *Al-Mufhim lima Ashkala min Talkhis Kitab Muslim*. 1st ed. Dar Ibn Kathir, n.d.

Sallam, Abu 'Ubaid al-Qasim b. al-. *Kitab Al-Amwal*. Muhammad Khalil. Cairo: Maktaba al-Kulliyyat al-Azhariyyah, 1388 AH.

Tabari, Abu Ja'far Muhammad b. Jarir al-. *Tahdhib al-Athar Musnad 'Ali Ibn Abi Talib*. Edited by Mahmud Muhammad Shakir. Cairo: Matba'a al-Madani, 1982 CE.

Tirmidhi, Muhammad b. 'Isa al-. *Jami' al-Tirmidhi*, n.p.

About Shaykh Muhammad al-Yaqoubi

SHAYKH MUHAMMAD AL-YAQOUBI is a world-renowned Islamic scholar of theology, jurisprudence, Prophetic tradition, and a spiritual leader to thousands of Muslims across the globe. He has been named one of the 500 most influential Muslims in the world for the past five years (theMuslim500.com).

Shaykh al-Yaqoubi was born in Damascus in 1963 and trained from an early age in the Islamic sciences by his father, who was an Imam and instructor at the Grand Umayyad Mosque in Damascus. Since the age of eleven, he has been continuously teaching the Islamic sciences and has been giving Friday sermons since the age of fourteen. He descends from a scholarly family that traces its lineage back to the Prophet Muhammad ﷺ. Three of his ancestors were also Imams at the Grand Umayyad Mosque.

A Sufi Master of the Shadhili Order, his primary focus is on the purification of the heart, the spiritual well-being of Muslims, and the rectification of their social conduct and interaction within society based on the highest virtues of the Prophet of Islam ﷺ.

He has travelled around the world teaching Muslims, and bringing awareness to and spreading moderate Islam. Thousands of students have studied under him, many of whom are now Imams and teachers in the Islamic World—in the Arab world, the West, the Far East, and South Africa.

Shaykh Al-Yaqoubi was one of the first scholars to speak up against the Assad regime and, subsequently, against the rise of ISIS, denouncing its atrocities and proving its actions to be un-Islamic. To this end, he has delivered numerous lectures, penned articles, and given several TV and paper interviews to media agencies such as CNN, BBC, and PBS.

He is the author of several books in Arabic in the areas of Islamic law and Prophetic Tradition.

He speaks Arabic, English, and Swedish, and reads French and German.

CAREER HIGHLIGHTS

1981–1990 Friday Imam, al-Tawusiyyah Mosque, Damascus

1983–1990 Instructor, al-Darwishiyah Mosque, the Fatwa Administration, Damascus, Syria

1986–1991 Teacher of Islamic law, the Institute of Shaykh Badr al-Din al-Hasani, Damascus, Syria

1992–1996 Researcher and teacher, Ph.D program of linguistics, Institute of Oriental Studies, University of Gothenburg, Sweden

1992–1996 Imam, Islamic Society of Gothenburg

1993–1998 Co-Founder of NCID - Nordic Centre for Inter-religious Dialogue, Gothenburg Sweden

1995 Member of an independent "Peace Mission to Sarajevo"" coordinated by the Swedish Foreign Department

1996 Winner of Peace Prize "Hagges Fredspris," Gothenburg, Sweden

1998–2000 Assistant director for research and studies at the Islamic museum of Kuwait, Dar al-Athar a-Islamiyyah, Kuwait

2000 Founding member of the Swedish Muslim Academy, Stockholm, Sweden

2006–2011 Lecturer in Sufism, Ibn Arabi Mosque, Damascus

2007– Patron of the educational organization Sacred Knowledge - UK and USA

2008–2011 Lecturer at the Grand Umayyad mosque, Damascus, Syria.

2008–2011 Friday Imam at al-Hassan mosque, Damascus, Syria

2008– Patron of the humanitarian relief organization SKT Welfare – UK and USA

2010–2011 Former member of the Supreme committee overseeing Islamic insurance companies and their compatibility with the Shariah

2010–2011 Member of the High Committee for reforming curricula of Islamic schools in Syria.

2012–2013 Guest Professor at Al-Akhawin University, Ifrane,

Morocco (teaching Jurisprudence, Philology and Exegesis of the Quran)

2014– Foundation Fellow, Muslim Faculty of Advanced Studies, Norwich, UK

2014– Patron, Al-Huda Center for Education & Counseling, Amman, Jordan